WITHDRAWN

61508

DATE			

WITHDRAWN

I.C.C. LIBRARY

© THE BAKER & TAYLOR CO.

SCOTT AND ERNEST

SCOTT
AND
ERNEST

The Authority of Failure
and the
Authority of Success

Matthew J. Bruccoli, 1931–

Random House · New York

Grateful acknowledgment is made to the following for permission to reprint previously published material:

Esquire, Inc.: Excerpts from "Scott, Ernest, and Whoever" by Arnold Gingrich. Quotations from the published writings of Ernest Hemingway are used with the permission of Mary Welsh Hemingway and are fully protected by copyright.

John F. Kennedy Library: Fitzgerald-to-Hemingway letters from the Ernest Hemingway Collection at the John F. Kennedy Library.

Harold Matson Co., Inc.: Excerpts from *That Summer in Paris* by Morley Callaghan. Copyright © 1963 by Morley Callaghan.

New Directions Publishing Corporation: *The Crack-Up* by F. Scott Fitzgerald. Copyright 1939 by Esquire, Inc. Copyright 1945 by New Directions Publishing Corporation.

Charles Scribner's Sons: Excerpts from *Dear Scott/Dear Max: The Fitzgerald-Perkins Correspondence*, edited by John Kuehl and Jackson Bryer. Copyright 1950, © 1971 by Charles Scribner's Sons. Copyright © 1963 by Frances Scott Fitzgerald Lanahan; quotations from the works of Ernest Hemingway are used with the permission of Charles Scribner's Sons, and are fully protected by copyright; excerpts from *The Letters of F. Scott Fitzgerald*, edited by Andrew Turnbull. Copyright © 1963 by Frances Scott Fitzgerald Lanahan.

Library of Congress Cataloging in Publication Data
Bruccoli, Matthew Joseph, 1931–
Scott and Ernest: the authority of failure and the
authority of success.
1.   Fitzgerald, Francis Scott Key, 1869–1940—Friends
and associates.   2.   Hemingway, Ernest, 1899–1961—
Friends and associates.   3.   Fitzgerald, Francis Scott
Key, 1896–1940—Correspondence.   4.   Hemingway, Ernest,
1899–1961—Correspondence.   I.   Title.
PS3511.I9Z565   813'.5'209 [B]   77-90250
ISBN 0-394-42889-7

Manufactured in the United States of America

2 4 6 8 9 7 5 3

First Edition

For Arlyn at Twenty

Acknowledgments

Although I didn't know it, this book began on the night of 24 June 1972, when Frazer Clark, James Jones, and I tried to visit all the bars mentioned in *The Sun Also Rises*. Our first stop was the Dingo (now the Bar Basque). In October 1976 I read a paper on the Fitzgerald/Hemingway relationship at the University of Alabama Hemingway Conference. Then I started writing *Scott and Ernest*.

My chief debts are to Scottie Fitzgerald Smith and Mary Welsh Hemingway for access to the evidence. Both of them read this book in typescript. Alexander Clark and the always-helpful staff at the Princeton University Library made it possible for me to work with the Fitzgerald Papers. Jo August, William Johnson, and Robert Stocking assisted my research in the Hemingway Papers at the Kennedy Library. Cara White asked many useful questions while typing this book. Charles Mann generously shared his Hemingway research with me. My Arlyn vetted the drafts and tried to remove the infelicities of style. Vernon Sternberg and Margaret Duggan made useful recommendations for improving the working draft. Susan Walker and Karen Rood helped with final preparation of the typescript. The late James Charters wrote me long letters about Paris in the old days. I am also obligated to Morrill Cody and Duncan Chaplin for searching their memories. Carlos Baker, Hemingway's biographer, patiently answered question after question. William Nolte, Head, Department of English, University of South Carolina, provided travel help at key points. Albert Erskine, my editor, always improves my work.

I am grateful to be at the University of South Carolina, where I can get my work done.

Matthew J. Bruccoli
19 March 1977

Chronology

Fall 1926: Hadley and Ernest separate.

22 October 1926: Publication of *The Sun Also Rises.*

December 1926: Fitzgeralds return to America.

January 1927: Fitzgerald goes to Hollywood to write "Lipstick" (unproduced) for United Artists.

March 1927–March 1929: Fitzgeralds rent "Ellerslie," near Wilmington, Delaware.

May 1927: Hemingway marries Pauline Pfeiffer.

14 October 1927: Publication of *Men Without Women.*

April–August 1928: Fitzgeralds spend spring and summer in Paris.

April 1928: Hemingways make first visit to Key West, Florida.

19–20 November 1928
Fitzgeralds and Hemingways attend Yale-Princeton football game at Princeton; the Hemingways spend the night at "Ellerslie."

6 December 1928
Fitzgerald delivers cash to Hemingway at North Philadelphia Station following the suicide of Dr. Hemingway.

March 1929: Fitzgeralds return to Europe.

May–October 1929: Serialization of *A Farewell to Arms* in *Scribner's Magazine.*

June 1929
Fitzgerald and Hemingway in Paris. Fitzgerald reads typescript of *A Farewell to Arms.*

June 1929
Hemingway and Callaghan box in Paris; Fitzgerald is timekeeper.

27 September 1929: Publication of *A Farewell to Arms.*

FITZGERALD	HEMINGWAY
	24 November 1929: Account of Hemingway-Callaghan bout appears in *New York Herald Tribune*.
April 1930: Zelda Fitzgerald has breakdown in Paris. In June she is placed at Prangins Clinic near Geneva.	
September 1931: Zelda Fitzgerald is released from Prangins. Fitzgeralds return to America permanently.	
September 1931–May 1932: Fitzgeralds rent a house in Montgomery, Alabama.	

October 1931
Fitzgerald and Hemingway meet—
probably in New York.

FITZGERALD	HEMINGWAY
December 1931: Fitzgerald goes to Hollywood to work on *Red-Headed Woman* at MGM.	
February 1932: Zelda Fitzgerald has second breakdown; is placed at Phipps Clinic of Johns Hopkins Hospital in Baltimore.	
May 1932–November 1933: Fitzgerald rents "La Paix" near Baltimore.	
	23 September 1932: Publication of *Death in the Afternoon*.
7 October 1932: Publication of Zelda Fitzgerald's novel, *Save Me the Waltz*.	

January 1933
Fitzgerald and Hemingway meet in New York.

FITZGERALD	HEMINGWAY
	27 October 1933: Publication of *Winner Take Nothing*.
	December 1933–February 1934: Hemingways on safari in Africa.

January–April 1934: Serialization of *Tender Is the Night* in *Scribner's Magazine.*

12 April 1934: Publication of *Tender Is the Night.*

May 1934: Zelda Fitzgerald's third breakdown.

October 1934: Publication of "In the Darkest Hour," the first Philippe story.

20 March 1935: Publication of *Taps at Reveille.*

                                       25 October 1935: Publication of *Green Hills of Africa.*

1935–1937: Fitzgerald in North Carolina, mostly staying at the Grove Park Inn, Asheville. The "crack-up" period.

April 6, 1936: Zelda Fitzgerald is placed in Highland Hospital, Asheville, N.C.

February 1936: Publication of "The Crack-Up" in *Esquire.*

August 1936
Publication of "The Snows of Kilimanjaro" in *Esquire.*

March 1937: Hemingway goes to Spain as war correspondent for NANA.

4 June 1937
Fitzgerald and Hemingway meet in New York when Hemingway addresses American Writers' Congress.

July 1937: Fitzgerald moves to Hollywood, under contract to MGM. Meets Sheilah Graham.

July 1937
Final meeting of Fitzgerald and Hemingway in Hollywood at showing of *The Spanish Earth.*

15 October 1937: Publication of *To Have and Have Not.*

FITZGERALD	HEMINGWAY
	14 October 1938: Publication of *The Fifth Column and The First Forty-Nine Stories.*
January 1939: Termination of Fitzgerald's MGM contract.	
Late summer 1939: Fitzgerald begins writing *The Last Tycoon.*	
	21 October 1940: Publication of *For Whom the Bell Tolls.*
	21 November 1940: Hemingway marriés Martha Gellhorn.
	December 1940: Hemingway buys the Finca Vigia, outside of Havana.
21 December 1940: Fitzgerald dies of a heart attack at Sheilah Graham's apartment, 1443 N. Hayworth, Hollywood.	
27 October 1941: Publication of *The Last Tycoon.*	
	May 1944–March 1945: Hemingway in London and France as *Collier's* correspondent.
12 August 1945: Publication of *The Crack-Up.*	
	14 March 1946: Hemingway marries Mary Welsh.

June 1947
Death of Maxwell Perkins.

FITZGERALD	HEMINGWAY
10 March 1948: Death of Zelda Fitzgerald in a fire at Highland Hospital.	
	7 September 1950: Publication of *Across the River and into the Trees.*
	8 September 1952: Publication of *The Old Man and the Sea.*
	October 1954: Hemingway is awarded the Nobel Prize.
	2 July 1961: Hemingway commits suicide in his home at Ketchum, Idaho.
	5 May 1964: Publication of *A Moveable Feast.*

SCOTT AND ERNEST

Introduction

The first time I ever met Scott Fitzgerald a very strange thing happened. Many strange things happened with Scott but this one I was never able to forget. He had come into the Dingo bar in the rue Delambre where I was sitting with some completely worthless characters, had introduced himself and introduced a tall, pleasant man who was with him as Dunc Chaplin, the famous pitcher. I had not followed Princeton baseball and had never heard of Dunc Chaplin but he was extraordinarily nice, un-worried, relaxed and friendly, and I much preferred him to Scott.

A Moveable Feast

Thus begins Ernest Hemingway's posthumously published account of his friendship with F. Scott Fitzgerald—which portrays Fitzgerald as a drunk, a weakling, a hypochondriac, an irresponsible writer, a nuisance, an embarrassment, as both sexually insecure and wife-dominated, and even questions Fitzgerald's taste in ties. It is a highly convincing recollection, utilizing Hemingway's reportorial skills and his "rat-trap memory" for details. Moreover, this first encounter is documented by a witness: Fitzgerald's Princeton friend Duncan Chaplin was there, too. But Chaplin was not in the Dingo bar on the rue Delambre that spring day in 1925. Chaplin was not in Paris. Chaplin was not even in Europe in 1925.[1]

Perhaps it was someone else—another Princetonian. But Chaplin is carefully identified as part of the sense of exact recall Hemingway develops in these memoirs. As the scene is set up, it has to be Chaplin. One wrong detail undermines the whole thing: all of it has to be right. Hemingway's error about Dunc Chaplin opens

---

1 After fifty years Duncan Chaplin has no recollection of ever having met Hemingway: "I left Genoa for home about Dec. 15–to Jan. 15–1920 & did not return to Paris after my short stay in 1919—" (to MJB, 26 November 1976). Chaplin served with the U.S. Naval aviation in Italy from August 1918 to the end of 1919. Since Hemingway was with the Red Cross in Italy from June 1918 to January 1919, it is possible that they met in Italy and that Hemingway's memory later moved Chaplin to the Dingo.

[3]

larger questions about the Fitzgerald/Hemingway relationship, for Hemingway is the only source for some of the most widely repeated anecdotes about Fitzgerald.

No one has ever really had total recall, and it is well to remember that Hemingway wrote *A Moveable Feast* more than thirty years after the events he reports. In 1956 the porters at the Paris Ritz reminded Hemingway that he had left two small trunks there in 1928, which turned out to be full of material from his early Paris days. This discovery had a catalytic effect on the writing of *A Moveable Feast;* but there is no evidence that any of the Paris sketches were salvaged from those trunks. The recollections were written between 1957 and 1960. Hemingway provided a warning in his Preface: "If the reader prefers, this book may be regarded as fiction. But there is always the chance that such a book of fiction may throw some light on what has been written as fact."

The best-known anecdote about Fitzgerald appears in Hemingway's 1936 story, "The Snows of Kilimanjaro": "He remembered poor Scott Fitzgerald and his romantic awe of them [the rich] and how he had started a story once about them that began 'The very rich are different from you and me.' And how someone had said to Scott, 'Yes they have more money.' But that was not humorous to Scott. He thought they were a special glamorous race and when he found they weren't it wrecked him just as much as any other thing that wrecked him." The only true thing in the passage is the quotation from Fitzgerald's story "The Rich Boy"—which did not begin the story. The rest never happened—or, at least, it didn't happen that way. In 1936 Maxwell Perkins, the legendary editor of Fitzgerald and Hemingway at Charles Scribner's Sons, lunched with Hemingway and the critic Mary Colum. When Hemingway announced, "I am getting to know the rich," Mary Colum replied, "The only difference between the rich and other people is that the rich have more money." The mechanism of Hemingway's reaction seems appallingly clear: a standard way to get rid of an embarrassment is to assign it to someone else. In this case "poor Scott," whose "Crack-Up" articles were appearing in *Esquire,* provided an easy target.

These instances in which Hemingway's testimony about Fitzgerald is demonstrably untrustworthy indicate that an examination of all the evidence in the Scott/Ernest case is required. Since some of the anecdotes about these two figures have become common-places of American literary history, the record should be set straight. There are excellent biographies of both Fitzgerald and Hemingway —particularly Carlos Baker's *Hemingway: A Life Story*—but in these volumes the focus is necessarily on the subject of the biog-raphy, so that the relationship between the two writers has not been fully scrutinized. A documentary reconstruction of their friendship and estrangement enlarges our understanding of these geniuses— especially of Hemingway, who became his own greatest creation.

There is no need to aggrandize either F. Scott Fitzgerald or Ernest Hemingway at the other's expense. Their works will endure for as long as books are read—which is all that really mattered to them. Partisans have been moved to make comparative judgments on Fitzgerald and Hemingway, attempting to defend the stature of one by diminishing the other. This procedure often adduces biographical evidence; but the personal relationship between Fitz-gerald and Hemingway has been mythologized. Things that never happened have been printed as facts. What did happen has been distorted.

The mortality rate among literary friendships is high. Writers tend to be bad risks as friends—probably for much the same reasons that they are bad matrimonial risks. They save the best parts of themselves for their work. Moreover, literary ambition has a way of turning into literary competition. If fame is the spur, envy may be a concomitant.

F. Scott Fitzgerald and Ernest Hemingway had great friend-ship needs. They both sought admiration and companionship. Hemingway needed an audience. Fitzgerald needed heroes. The cadre of Hemingway's literary ex-friends is impressive; and his feuds with them were often conducted in print or in public—as he broke with Sherwood Anderson, Gertrude Stein, John Dos Passos, Archibald MacLeish, Donald Ogden Stewart, Robert Mc-Almon, Ford Madox Ford, Morley Callaghan, Harold Loeb, Max Eastman, and Ernest Walsh. Examining the pattern of Heming-way's friendships—especially during his apprentice period—makes it difficult to avoid the conclusion that young Hemingway had a compulsion to declare his independence from, or non-indebtedness to, writers who could be said to have helped or influenced him. Few of Hemingway's writer-friends managed to stay the distance: Ezra Pound, James Joyce, and—in a special way—F. Scott Fitzgerald. Hemingway never saw Pound after 1924. Hemingway and Joyce were not close friends. Fitzgerald maintained the outward forms of friendship with Hemingway for fifteen years, until his death in 1940.

I

The first mention of either man by the other came in Fitzgerald's October 1924 letter to Maxwell Perkins of Scribners, written from St. Raphaël on the Riviera, where he was completing *The Great Gatsby*. Acting as volunteer literary scout, Fitzgerald wrote: "This is to tell you about a young man named Ernest Hemmingway, who lives in Paris, (an American) writes for the transatlantic Review + has a brilliant future. Ezra Pount published a collection of his short pieces in Paris, at some place like the Egotist Press, I haven't it hear now but its remarkable + I'd look him up right away. He's the real thing."[2] It is characteristic of Fitzgerald that although his recommendation is full of errors (he would never master the spelling of *Hemingway*), it is right about the important matter: Hemingway was the real thing. The volume to which Fitzgerald reacted so strongly was *in our time,* published in Paris by the Three Mountains Press in a series, "*The Inquest* into the state of contemporary English prose," edited by Ezra Pound. This 32-page book (actually a pamphlet bound in stiff covers) was limited to 170 copies and consisted of eighteen vignettes that were later used as the interchapters in Hemingway's first story collection, *In Our Time* (New York; Boni & Liveright, 1925). The connection between Fitzgerald

[2] The documents quoted in this book are printed as written.

Villa Marie,
Valescure
St. Raphael, France

Dear Max:
        The royalty was better than I'd
expected. This is to tell you about a
young man named Ernest Hemmingway,
who lives in Paris, (an American) writes
for the transatlantic Review + has a
brilliant future. Ezra Pound published a
a collection of his short pieces in Paris,
at some place like the Egotist Press, I
haven't it here now but its remarkable
+ I'd look him up right away. He's
the real thing.

Charles Scribner's Sons Papers, Princeton University Library.

and Hemingway was provided by Edmund Wilson, Fitzgerald's
Princeton friend who was establishing himself as one of the most
brilliant American literary critics. in our time was published in
March 1924, before the Fitzgeralds moved to France, and Wilson
called Scott's attention to it. Wilson receptively reviewed Hemingway's first two Paris publications, *Three Stories & Ten Poems*
(Paris: Contact Press, 1923—300 copies) and *in our time* (Paris:
Three Mountains Press, 1924—170 copies) in the October 1924
issue of *The Dial*. Although Fitzgerald did not cite Wilson to Perkins, the *Dial* review appeared the same month that Fitzgerald
wrote Perkins.

        By October 1924 Hemingway had achieved five nonjournalis-
tic magazine appearances in America: a fable and a poem in *The
Double Dealer*, six poems in *Poetry*, a poem and six vignettes in
The Little Review. *The Best Short Stories of 1923* included the
previously unpublished "My Old Man" in a volume that was dedicated to "Ernest Hemenway"; but the story didn't attract much attention. Hemingway's luck was no better in the expatriate maga-

[8]

THREE STORIES

Up in Michigan
Out of Season
My Old Man

& TEN POEMS

Mitraigliatrice
Oklahoma
Oily Weather
Roosevelt
Captives
Champs d'Honneur
Riparto d'Assalto
Montparnasse
Along With Youth
Chapter Heading

*To Phillip
Jordan
Hommages
Respecteeus ox
Pron
Ernest H. Emingway
Paris October 1925*

ERNEST HEMINGWAY

the author   *wood-cut from portrait by henry strater*

in our time
by
ernest hemingway

A GIRL IN CHICAGO: Tell us about
the French women, Hank. What are
they like?
BILL SMITH: How old are the French
women, Hank?

paris:
*printed at the three mountains press and for sale
at shakespeare & company, in the rue de l'odéon;
london: william jackson, took's court, curaine street, chancery lane.*
1924

zines, where only one of his short stories, "Indian Camp," and two articles had appeared in the *Transatlantic Review* before October 1924. Hemingway had, however, achieved the two separate publications in Paris. Fitzgerald may not have read *3 & 10*[3] when he wrote Perkins. If he had, his recommendation might have been even stronger, for the three stories were "Up in Michigan," "Out of Season," and "My Old Man." As it was, Fitzgerald's prediction of Hemingway's "brilliant future" was prescient, for it was based on only the vignettes of *in our time,* which provided no more than samples of Hemingway's style and tone:

> We were in a garden in Mons. Young Buckley came in with his patrol from across the river. The first German I saw climbed up over the garden wall. We waited till he got one leg over and then potted him. He had so much equipment on and looked awfully surprised and fell down into the garden. Then three more came over further down the wall. We shot them. They all came just like that.

The hallmarks of the great Hemingway style are here: the clear diction, the abrupt rhythm, the absence of transitions between sentences, the "and" constructions, the reliance on simple declarative sentences, the controlled understatement, the concern with violence. But to predict a "brilliant future" for the writer of eighteen vignettes—the longest of which is less than 350 words—was reckless. It is possible that Fitzgerald may have heard through the literary grapevine something more about Hemingway, who had already attracted attention beyond his actual achievement as a literary contender. As the author of two little books, which were virtually privately published with a total of 470 copies, Hemingway was already regarded as the most promising young American writer in Paris. The word could have filtered down to St. Raphaël.

Through fall 1924–spring 1925 Fitzgerald continued to remind Perkins about Hemingway while revising *The Great Gatsby* in Rome and Capri. Perkins was unable to find a copy of *in our time* until February 1925, at which time he wrote Hemingway

[3] At his death Fitzgerald's library included a copy of *Three Stories & Ten Poems,* but it is impossible to determine where or when he acquired it.

expressing interest in publishing him; but Perkins did not have his current address. In late April 1925 Fitzgerald was in Paris, where he sought out Hemingway. Their first meeting at the Dingo occurred before 1 May; on that date Fitzgerald wrote Perkins that Hemingway had signed a contract with Boni & Liveright for *In Our Time.*

In the spring of 1925 Ernest Hemingway, who was not yet twenty-six, was living with his wife Hadley and their son John (called "Bumby") on the Left Bank. Born in 1899 the son of a doctor in Oak Park, Illinois, he grew up in a solidly middle-class, conservative, pious family. After graduating from Oak Park High School in 1917 he worked for six months as a cub reporter on the *Kansas City Star* before going to Italy in 1918 as an ambulance driver with the American Red Cross. He was wounded and fell in love with a nurse, who declined to marry him. After the war he unsuccessfully tried to write fiction before returning to journalism in Chicago and Toronto. In September 1921 Hemingway married Hadley Richardson, who was seven years older than he.

By Christmas the Hemingways were in Paris, where he wrote articles for the *Toronto Star* at space rates. He was not on salary; the paper paid him for what it printed. At that time he impressed new acquaintances as shy and sincere. He made friends easily, for at every stage of his career he possessed great vitality and magnetism. His dedication to writing was real and absolutely convincing. Among his early friends and benefactors in Paris were Ezra Pound, Gertrude Stein, and two publishers, Robert McAlmon and William Bird. Sylvia Beach, proprietress of the Shakespeare & Co. bookshop on the rue de l'Odéon and publisher of James Joyce's *Ulysses,* remained a lifelong friend. Although she did not publish his work, Beach was a widely liked figure in the Paris literary world, and her good will helped Hemingway. When the Hemingways returned to Toronto for the birth of their child in September 1923, *Three Stories & Ten Poems* had been published by McAlmon and *in our time* had been accepted for publication by Bird. Hemingway worked as a reporter on the *Toronto Star* until December 1923, when he quit his job because his boss was harassing him and because he couldn't get on with his own writing in Toronto. In January 1924 the Hemingways were back in Paris and living over a sawmill at 113 rue Notre Dame des Champs off the Boulevard Montparnasse.

Hemingway's accounts of his Paris apprenticeship from 1922 to 1926 are full of dedication and poverty. The dedication was authentic, but the poverty was largely illusory. Hadley was a small heiress. At the time of their marriage she had an income of $3000 a year from a trust fund. Americans could live well in Paris in 1922 on $3000, for the rate of exchange was favorable. Although Hadley's income was later reduced by the mismanagement of the trustee, the Hemingways were not paupers and did not have to rely on his earnings for eating money. There was always money for the things Hemingway wanted to do. Their apartments lacked plumbing, but when they lived at 74 rue Cardinale Lemoine in 1922–23, Hemingway was able to rent a room nearby to write in. "Hunger was good discipline," he claimed in *A Moveable Feast;* nonetheless, they could afford trips to Spain for the bullfights and long stays in the Austrian alps when he found it difficult to work during the rainy winters in Paris. There was even money to gamble on the horses—surely a losing proposition, despite Hemingway's confidence in his handicapping skill.

In the spring of 1925, Fitzgerald, who was not yet twenty-nine, was living with his wife Zelda and their daughter Scottie at 14 rue de Tilsitt, near the Arc de Triomphe. Born in 1896, Fitzgerald had been raised in St. Paul, Minnesota. His father was a business failure, and the family lived on Mrs. Fitzgerald's modest inheritance. Fitzgerald was keenly aware of his position as a poor boy at rich-boy schools. After Newman, a Catholic prep school in New Jersey, he entered Princeton with the class of 1917. In constant academic difficulties, he had to repeat a year. He left Princeton in 1918 to take an Army commission. After his discharge from the Army in 1919 Fitzgerald tried to make a quick success in New York advertising in order to marry Zelda Sayre, the Alabama belle he had fallen in love with while stationed near Montgomery. When Zelda proved unwilling to wait and broke their engagement, Fitzgerald quit his job and rewrote the novel he had written in the Army. Published by Scribners, *This Side of Paradise* was a surprise success in 1920, selling 40,000 copies in its first year. The money poured

Ernest and Hadley Hemingway in Switzerland.

in, for Fitzgerald was a skilled writer of short stories for the slick magazines. His income in 1920, his first full year as a professional writer, was $18,500—which had the purchasing power of perhaps $50,000 now. He needed it. Scott and Zelda were married in April 1920 and embarked on an extravagant life. Fitzgerald became a newspaper celebrity and tried to live up to it, acquiring a reputation as the playboy of American literature. In the late spring of 1924 the Fitzgeralds went to the Riviera—then unfashionable in warm months—to live quietly and economize while he wrote *The Great Gatsby*. They were incapable of economizing, but the novel was finished in the fall. Fitzgerald had hoped that *Gatsby* would make enough money so that he could give up short stories and concentrate on writing novels. The reviews were excellent, but the sales were disappointing: Scribners sold fewer than 23,000 copies in 1925.

When F. Scott Fitzgerald entered the Dingo—without Dunc Chaplin—that April day in 1925 he was the author of *This Side of Paradise* (1920), *The Beautiful and Damned* (1922), and *The Great Gatsby* (1925), as well as two volumes of stories, *Flappers and Philosophers* (1920) and *Tales of the Jazz Age* (1922). Ernest Hemingway was the author of *Three Stories & Ten Poems* (1923) and *in our time* (1924)—a total of eighty-eight printed pages. Yet from the inception of their friendship there was a role reversal. The literary apprentice awed the famous author. In addition to his admiration for Hemingway's talent, Fitzgerald was impressed by two aspects of the already evolving Hemingway legend—by his reputation as a war hero and an athlete.

Fitzgerald, who did not get overseas in World War I, felt that he had missed a test of manhood and worried about how he would have behaved in battle. The war was very much on his mind in the Twenties. He studied books about the Great War, collected stereopticon slides of the battlefields, and was fascinated by pictures of mutilated soldiers. Hemingway was reputedly an authentic war hero who had been wounded while serving with the Red Cross in Italy and had then fought with the Arditti, an elite corps of Italian shock troops. In actuality he had never been in combat. He had been wounded by a mortar while distributing candy and cigarettes in July 1918, and had been hit by machine-gun fire while carrying another wounded man. At the time of the Armistice he was still undergoing treatment in Milan. Nonetheless, Hemingway was known in Paris as a combat veteran, a reputation which he did not discourage.

Fitzgerald was a disappointed athlete who said that he had sought literary recognition at school to compensate for his failure at football. Here again, Hemingway impressed him with his reputation as an athlete. In point of fact, the only athletic event in which Hemingway had distinguished himself at Oak Park High School was the plunge—a flat distance dive. Big but clumsy, he did win a letter in football. He excelled at fishing and hunting and assiduously developed his reputation as a boxer. His boxing enhanced the Hemingway image as it was reported that, disgusted with the conduct of one of the fighters at a professional match, he had climbed into the ring and knocked out the fighter. He claimed that he had been trained by professional fighters in Chicago as a boy, had worked as a sparring partner, and had been a bouncer in tough joints in America. There is no evidence to support any of this. Hemingway boxed for exercise regularly in Paris—often with inexperienced people like Ezra Pound—and set himself up as a boxing master. On 19 October 1925 he reported to his mother that he was earning extra money giving boxing lessons, and that Scott Fitzgerald was one of his pupils. Hemingway did look like an athlete. At six feet and 190 pounds he was a big man for that time, and seemed bigger. At five eight Fitzgerald was too small for football. Although he had won his letter at Newman, he was cut from the Princeton freshman squad after the first day of practice because they didn't need 140-pound halfbacks.

Hemingway's *A Moveable Feast* is the only source for their first meeting at the Dingo. Indeed, it is the only record that the meeting did take place at the Dingo. He describes Fitzgerald's looks as "between handsome and pretty" and makes an ominous comment on his feminine mouth. Hemingway acknowledges that he himself was with "some completely worthless characters"—implying it is permissible to drink with "completely worthless characters" if you know that they are "completely worthless." Fitzgerald begins complimenting his work, which annoys Hemingway because he believes that "praise to the face is open disgrace." Instead

[15]

F. Scott Fitzgerald
Novelist.

Mr. F. Scott Fitzgerald is popularly credited with the discovery of the flapper. Whether he did that or not,

of listening to Fitzgerald, Hemingway studies him and notices that he is wearing a Brooks Brothers button-down shirt and a Guards tie. (This tie has one-inch diagonal stripes of navy blue and dark red; it can be legitimately worn by all ranks of the Brigade of Guards, which consists of the five regiments of Foot Guards as well as the Household Cavalry.) Hemingway considers warning Fitzgerald that his tie might cause him embarrassment with British visitors in Paris. There were two in the Dingo just then. Later in the recollection it develops that they were almost certainly Duff Twysden and Pat Guthrie, the Lady Brett and Mike Campbell of *The Sun Also Rises*. If so, did it matter what a couple of "completely worthless" drunks thought about F. Scott Fitzgerald's tie? It was uncharacteristic for Hemingway to be clothes-conscious. In those days, he made a point of being superior to clothes, wearing sweatshirts and patched pants. Fitzgerald, though never a dandy, was a well-dressed man.

Hemingway does not drop the matter of the tie—which he notes Fitzgerald bought in Rome. At their next meeting a couple of days later at the Closerie de Lilas cafe on the Place St. Michel, Hemingway brings up the tie. When Fitzgerald claims that he left the Dingo because he got fed up with Hemingway's British friends —"that girl with the phony title who was so rude and that silly drunk with her"—Hemingway at first insists that there hadn't been any British there. Then Hemingway asks him if they had been rude about his tie. He reports that Fitzgerald was puzzled by this concern about his tie, saying that he was "wearing a plain black knitted tie with a white polo shirt." No matter what the tie was, the picture of Fitzgerald wearing any tie with a polo shirt is ludicrous. A polo shirt is a knit shirt, usually worn open at the neck. But at that time Brooks Brothers shirts had three collar styles called golf, tennis, and polo. The polo collar was the classic button-down collar, which Fitzgerald wore. Hemingway conveys the impression that Fitzgerald was either wearing a tie with a polo shirt, or worse, wearing a Guards tie and thereby running the risk of outraging Duff Twysden and Pat Guthrie.

During the meeting at the Dingo, Fitzgerald annoys Hemingway by asking whether he had slept with his wife before they were married. This is probably an accurate report; there is confirmation

that Fitzgerald asked this question of new acquaintances. Then Fitzgerald passes out, which is also probably accurate. Fitzgerald, one of the legendary alcoholics of American letters, in fact had a low capacity for liquor. (Medical opinion now holds that he had hypoglycemia or hyperinsulinism.) There is ample supporting evidence for Hemingway's reports of Fitzgerald's drinking style. Hemingway had a great capacity for alcohol. He could drink after his daily writing stint and work the next day. Fitzgerald could undertake extended writing projects only when he was on the wagon.

At the Closerie de Lilas, Fitzgerald behaves well and Hemingway finds him endearing—"even if you were careful about anyone becoming endearing." Hemingway even allows himself to be impressed by Fitzgerald's non-conceited pride in *The Great Gatsby,* which had recently been published. But Hemingway undercuts Fitzgerald's achievement by belittling Gilbert Seldes' admiring review of the novel: "It could only have been better if Gilbert Seldes had been better." This review in the August 1925 *Dial,* which placed Fitzgerald ahead of all the writers "of his own generation and most of his elders," rankled Hemingway. (Hemingway could not have seen the August *Dial* in May, but it is possible that Seldes had sent Fitzgerald a typescript of the review.) One phrase particularly bothered him. Seldes praised *Gatsby* for "regarding a tiny section of life and reporting it with irony and pity and a consuming passion." When he wrote *The Sun Also Rises* Hemingway built in a scene in which Bill Gorton sings: "Irony and Pity. When you're feeling. . . . Oh, Give them Irony and Give them Pity. Oh, give them Irony. When they're feeling . . . Just a little irony. Just a little pity. . . ." Something more than envy was involved. *The Dial* was on Hemingway's shit-list, and he nurtured a lasting grudge against Gilbert Seldes because the magazine had declined his work while Seldes was the managing editor. Hemingway insisted that Seldes had written him a letter advising him to stick to journalism, but Seldes always denied it.

After Fitzgerald has shown that he could behave himself at the Closerie de Lilas, Hemingway accepts his invitation to go with him to Lyons to pick up the Fitzgeralds' car—at Fitzgerald's expense. Hemingway is looking forward to useful conversations with a successful writer, but is "shocked" to hear Fitzgerald admit that he changed his good stories for submission to *The Saturday Evening Post.* When Hemingway protests against this "whoring," Fitzgerald assures him that it did not damage his talent because he wrote the real story first. There is no evidence in the extensive Fitzgerald manuscript archive of a story in which this process occurred; but it is possible that he did make the claim to Hemingway. Fitzgerald regretted the expenditure of creative energy that went into his stories and frequently disparaged them.

In *A Moveable Feast* Hemingway recounts the Lyons trip in

detail. When Fitzgerald fails to show up at the train, Hemingway goes to Lyons alone, hoping to meet him there. Fitzgerald arrives the next morning and wastes a lot of time. The car has been badly abused by Fitzgerald, who has driven it without adding oil or water, and by Zelda Fitzgerald, who had the top removed. They start for Paris and are soaked by rain. Fitzgerald insists that he is in danger of dying from lung congestion. Hemingway has to nurse him and fakes taking his temperature with a large bath thermometer. Fitzgerald worries because he is spending his first night away from his wife—which was not true—and tells Hemingway about her affair with a French aviator at St. Raphaël, a story that Fitzgerald would repeat to him in other versions. At dinner Fitzgerald passes out from drink. The next day they drive to Paris while Fitzgerald discourses on Michael Arlen, and Hemingway invents a pretext to limit Fitzgerald's drinking. Fitzgerald did not regard the Lyons excursion as a disaster, for he later listed it in his *Notebooks* as among his "Most Pleasant Trips." In June Fitzgerald informed Gertrude Stein, "Hemmingway and I went to Lyons . . . to get my car and had a slick drive through Burgundy. He's a peach of a fellow and absolutely first-rate."

A few days later Fitzgerald brings Hemingway a copy of *The Great Gatsby*. Hemingway is embarrassed by the "violence, bad taste and slippery look" of the dust jacket; but Fitzgerald explains that the jacket "had to do with a billboard along a highway in Long Island that was important to the story." *Gatsby* has been greatly admired as an example of dust-jacket art, which is a matter of taste. What is not disputable is what the jacket shows. It does not show a billboard. The jacket has a woman's face over an amusement park night scene. After removing the offensive jacket, Hemingway reads *The Great Gatsby* and is so impressed that he vows to forgive Fitzgerald for his bad behavior: "When I had finished the book I knew that no matter what Scott did, nor how he behaved, I must know it was like a sickness and be of any help I could to him and try to be a good friend."

"Hawks Do Not Share," the second Fitzgerald sketch in *A Moveable Feast*, introduces Zelda Fitzgerald at "a very bad lunch" in the Fitzgeralds' "gloomy" apartment. From the start there was mutual distrust between Hemingway and Zelda Fitzgerald—

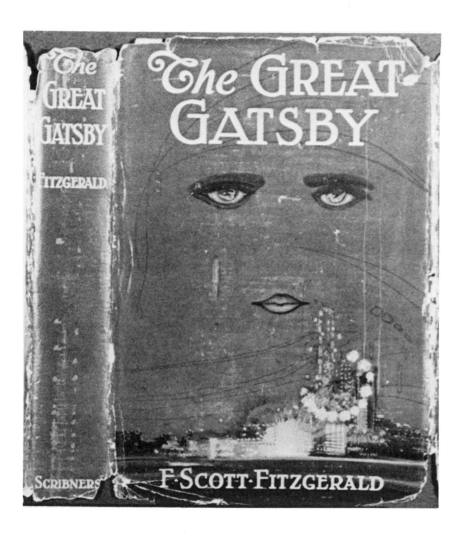

which developed into antagonism. Hemingway, who had lost his respect for his once-admired father as he saw him yield to a dominating wife, compensated for his father's weakness in his own marriage. The Hemingways did what Ernest wanted to do, and his work always came first. He was disgusted by Zelda's influence over Fitzgerald and by what he regarded as her deliberate interference with Fitzgerald's work. Zelda Fitzgerald may not have regarded Hemingway as a threat to her dominion, but she was immune to his charm and had reservations about his character. "Bogus" was one of her judgments on him, amplified with "materialistic mystic," "phony he-man," and "pansy with hair on his chest."

Hemingway was sure that Zelda Fitzgerald encouraged her husband's drinking to keep him from writing. Moreover, Hemingway reports that she was seeking out Lesbian company as part of her scheme to impede Fitzgerald's work. "Scott was afraid for her to pass out in the company they kept that spring and the places they went to. . . . Zelda did not encourage the people who were chasing her and she had nothing to do with them, she said. But it amused her and it made Scott jealous and he had to go with her to the places. It destroyed his work, and she was more jealous of his work than anything." Hemingway claims to have been the first to realize that Zelda Fitzgerald was insane, when, during the summer of 1926 on the Riviera, she asked him, "Ernest, don't you think Al Jolson is greater than Jesus?"

There were some good times that spring in Paris, despite the perilous undercurrents in the Fitzgerald marriage. Hemingway took Fitzgerald to 27 rue de Fleurus, where Fitzgerald charmed Gertrude Stein, who was impressed by his writing. "Fitzgerald was the only one of the younger writers who wrote naturally in sentences. . . . She thinks Fitzgerald will be read when many of his well-known contemporaries are forgotten," Stein later recorded in *The Autobiography of Alice B. Toklas.* Dean Christian Gauss of Princeton was in Paris during the spring of 1925, and Fitzgerald took considerable pride in setting up seminar-lunches at which he discussed literary topics with Hemingway and Gauss.

II

One way to gauge their friendship is from the letters F. Scott Fitzgerald and Ernest Hemingway wrote each other. On this evidence Hemingway emerges as a better friend than his self-portrait in *A Moveable Feast* shows—*until 1936*. Both were savers. Fifty-four pieces of their correspondence have been located—twenty-eight from Fitzgerald and twenty-six from Hemingway. Most of Fitzgerald's end of the correspondence has been published, but none of Hemingway's letters to Fitzgerald has been printed in its entirety. Since Hemingway's widow and executrix is honoring his prohibition of the publication of his letters, they will not be available in the near future. Mrs. Hemingway has generously permitted phrases from Hemingway's letters to be published in this book.

The first two letters in the series set the tone for much of the correspondence. Hemingway dominates and Fitzgerald defers. On 1 July 1925 Hemingway, en route to Pamplona and the Fiesta of San Fermín that would provide the material for *The Sun Also Rises* (1926), wrote a three-page letter from Burguete joking about Scott's drinking and sexual standards: "I wonder what your idea of heaven would be—A beautiful vacuum filled with wealthy monogamists all powerful and members of the best families all drinking themselves to death." Ernest's own idea of heaven would be a bull ring, a private trout stream, two houses in town—one for his wife and children and one for his mistresses—and a bull ranch. In the town houses *The Dial, The American Mercury,* and *The New Republic* would be used for toilet paper. On his way to the bull ranch he would toss coins to his illegitimate children and would send his son to town to lock the chastity belts on the mistresses because Scott Fitzgerald was in the area.

The first surviving letter from Fitzgerald—postmarked 30 November 1925—is, characteristically, an apology.

14 Rue de Tilsitt
Dear Ernest: I was quite ashamed the other morning. Not only in disturbing Hadly, but in foistering that "Juda Lincoln" alias George Morgenthau apon you. However it is only fair to say that the deplorable man who entered your appartment Sat. morning *was not* me but a man named Johnston who has often been mistaken for me.

Zelda, evidences to the contrary, was not suffering from lack of care but from a nervous hysteria which is only releived by a doctor bearing morphine. We both went to Ballau Wood next day to recuperate.

For some reason I told you a silly lie—or rather an exageration, silly because the truth itself was enough to make me sufficiently jubilant. The Sat. Eve. Post. raised me to $2750.00 and not $3000. which is a jump of $750. in one month. It was probably in my mind that I could now get $3000. from the smaller magazines. The *Post* merely met the Hearst offer, but that is something they seldom do.

What garbled versions of the McAlmon episode or the English orgy we lately participated in, I told you, I don't know. It is true that I saved McAlmon from a beating he probably deserved and that we went on some wild parties in London with a certain Marchioness of Milford Haven whom we first met with Telulah Bankhead. She was about half royalty, I think. Anyhow she was very nice—anything else I may have added about the relations between the Fitzgeralds and the house of Windsor is pure fiction.

I'm crazy to read the comic novel [*The Torrents of*

EDWARD J. O'BRIEN

"I regard this volume of short stories as a permanent contribution to the American literature of our time—a brave book not only for us but for posterity."

SHERWOOD ANDERSON

"Mr. Hemingway is young, strong, full of laughter, and he can write. His people flash suddenly up into those odd elusive moments of glowing reality, the clear putting down of which has always made good writing so good."

IN OUR TIME
BY ERNEST HEMINGWAY

GILBERT SELDES

"Extraordinary in its vividness and its brutality, it is, for the most part, deliberately unliterary, in the modern style. I can see it being warmly admired as I admire it, and violently disliked as I dislike some of it. But it has too much character, too much vital energy and passion to leave anyone indifferent. To me that is a high recommendation."

DONALD OGDEN STEWART

"After trying to make a meal out of the literary lettuce sandwiches which are being fed to this country, it is rather nice to discover that one of your own countrymen has opened a shop where you can really get something to eat."

WALDO FRANK

"Not in a long time have I been so impressed by the work of a new American author. Mr. Hemingway can write. His stories are hard, passionate bits of life."

FORD MADOX FORD

"The best writer in America at this moment (though for the moment he happens to be in Paris), the most conscientious, the most master of his craft, the most consummate, is Ernest Hemingway."

Spring]. Are you going to the Mclieshe's Tuesday? I hope
Hadly is well now. Please believe that we send our
Best Wishes to
Ernest M. Hemminway

Hemingway's first American book, *In Our Time,* was published by Boni & Liveright on 5 October 1925 in a first printing of 1335 copies. This collection of stories included "Indian Camp," "The Doctor and the Doctor's Wife," "The End of Something," "The Three-Day Blow," "The Battler," "A Very Short Story," "Soldier's Home," "The Revolutionist," "Mr. & Mrs. Elliot," "Cat in the Rain," "Out of Season," "Cross Country Snow," "My Old Man," and "Big Two-Hearted River"—as well as the vignettes from the 1924 Paris *in our time.* It was a strong volume, perhaps the most promising first volume of stories by an American; but story collections by unknown writers do not sell. Boni & Liveright was investing in Hemingway's future. A second printing was not needed until March 1927—after the success of *The Sun Also Rises.* The dust jacket for *In Our Time* had a display of blurbs by Sherwood Anderson, Gilbert Seldes, Donald Ogden Stewart, Waldo Frank, Edward J. O'Brien, and Ford Madox Ford—who called Hemingway "the best writer in America." Hemingway later broke with all of them, except O'Brien. Fitzgerald's review-essay, which did not appear in *The Bookman* until May 1926, was entitled "How to Waste Material: A Note on My Generation." After a long discussion of the failure of American writers to deal honestly with American material, he turns to Hemingway.

"In Our Time" consists of fourteen stories, short and long, with fifteen vivid miniatures interpolated between them. When I try to think of any contemporary American short stories as good as "Big Two-Hearted River", the last one in the book, only Gertrude Stein's "Melanctha", Anderson's "The Egg", and Lardner's "Golden Honeymoon" come to mind. It is the account of a boy on a fishing trip—he hikes, pitches his tent, cooks dinner, sleeps, and next morning casts for trout. Nothing more—but I read it with the most breathless unwilling interest I have experienced since Conrad first bent my reluctant eyes upon the sea.

The hero, Nick, runs through nearly all the stories, until the book takes on almost an autobiographical tint—in fact "My Old Man", one of the two in which this element seems entirely absent, is the least successful of all. Some of the stories show influences but they are invariably absorbed and transmuted, while in "My Old Man" there is an echo of Anderson's way of thinking in those sentimental "horse stories", which inaugurated his respectability and also his decline four years ago.

But with "The Doctor and the Doctor's Wife", "The End of Something", "The Three Day Blow", "Mr. and Mrs. Elliot", and "Soldier's Home" you are immediately aware of something temperamentally new. In the first of these a man is backed down by a half breed Indian after committing himself to a fight. The quality of humiliation in the story is so intense that it immediately calls up every such incident in the reader's past. Without the aid of a comment or a pointing finger one knows exactly the sharp emotion of young Nick who watches the scene.

The next two stories describe an experience at the last edge of adolescence. You are constantly aware of the continual snapping of ties that is going on around Nick. In the half stewed, immature conversation before the fire you watch the awakening of that vast unrest that descends upon the emotional type at about eighteen. Again there is not a single recourse to exposition. As in "Big Two-Hearted River", a picture—sharp, nostalgic, tense—develops before your eyes. When the picture is complete a light seems to snap out, the story is over. There is no tail, no sudden change of pace at the end to throw into relief what has gone before.

Nick leaves home penniless; you have a glimpse of him lying wounded in the street of a battered Italian town, and later of a love affair with a nurse on a hospital roof in Milan. Then in one of the best of the stories he is home again. The last glimpse of him is when his mother asks him, with all the bitter world in his heart, to kneel down beside her in the dining room in Puritan prayer.

Anyone who first looks through the short interpolated sketches will hardly fail to read the stories themselves. "The Garden at Mons" and "The Barricade" are profound essays upon the English officer, written on a postage stamp. "The

King of Greece's Tea Party", "The Shooting of the Cabinet Ministers", and "The Cigar-store Robbery" particularly fascinated me, as they did when Edmund Wilson first showed them to me in an earlier pamphlet, over two years ago.

Disregard the rather ill considered blurbs upon the cover. It is sufficient that here is no raw food served up by the railroad restaurants of California and Wisconsin. In the best of these dishes there is not a bit to spare. And many of us who have grown weary of admonitions to "watch this man or that" have felt a sort of renewal of excitement at these stories wherein Ernest Hemingway turns a corner into the street.

Hemingway now felt that Boni & Liveright was not the right publisher for him. Fitzgerald wanted him for Scribners, and Hemingway continued to correspond with Maxwell Perkins after signing with Boni & Liveright. On 9 June 1925 he wrote Perkins calling *Gatsby* "an absolutely first rate book." But Hemingway seemed tied up. His contract for *In Our Time* gave Boni & Liveright the option on his next three books, which would lapse only if the publisher declined the book submitted after *In Our Time*.

In the summer of 1925—while awaiting publication of *In Our Time*—Hemingway began a novel based on the Fiesta of San Fermín at Pamplona, which every year occupies a week in early July and was his favorite bull-fighting event. As usual, he organized his own mob for the 1925 trip: in addition to Hadley, he brought along Lady Duff Twysden, an alcoholic and promiscuous English remittance woman; Pat Guthrie, an alcoholic Scottish remittance man who was her fiancé-lover; Harold Loeb, an American writer who had recently enjoyed an affair with Duff; Bill Smith, Ernest's boyhood friend from northern Michigan; and humorist Donald Ogden Stewart. The Duff-Guthrie-Loeb mix promised awkwardness—if not worse—and the promise was fulfilled as Hemingway became disgusted by Loeb's conduct and turned nasty. Whether Hemingway was also jealous because Loeb had slept with Duff remains a matter for speculation. These people were all clearly identifiable in *The Sun Also Rises*. Duff Twysden is Brett Ashley; Pat Guthrie is Mike Campbell; Harold Loeb is Robert Cohn; and Smith and Stewart were amalgamated in Bill Gorton. Hemingway began writing the novel in Spain on 21 July 1925—his twenty-sixth birthday—and finished the first draft in Paris on 21 September. Before rewriting the novel, he wrote in one week during November a parody of Sherwood Anderson, *The Torrents of Spring*, which he submitted to Boni & Liveright in December 1925 as the second book under his contract.

Anderson's short stories had impressed and influenced Hemingway during his apprentice days. They had been friendly in Chicago in 1921, before the Hemingways went to Paris, and Anderson had encouraged the aspiring writer. One of Hemingway's first good stories, "My Old Man," shows Anderson's influence. Hemingway regarded Anderson's 1925 novel, *Dark Laughter,* as pretentious and faked. In *The Torrents of Spring* he undertook to provide corrective parody—as Henry Fielding had done by writing *Shamela* and *Joseph Andrews* in response to Samuel Richardson's *Pamela*. Since Anderson was the current star author of Boni & Liveright, the suspicion that Hemingway wrote *Torrents* to break his contract is inescapable; but he always denied it. Related to this point is the question of whether Fitzgerald was a co-conspirator, since he wanted Hemingway to join Maxwell Perkins' Scribners stable with him. A recently discovered Fitzgerald letter indicates that he and Hemingway had not hatched a scheme to use *Torrents* as a contract-breaker. Writing to Horace Liveright and Boni & Liveright editor T. R. Smith, Fitzgerald tried to persuade them to publish *Torrents*:

> 14 Rue de Tilsitt
> Paris
>
> Dear Horace and Tom:
>
> Ernest Hemminway showed me his new book the other day (the satiric book: *The Torrents of Spring*) and seemed a bit in doubt as to how you were going to recieve it. I don't know how much value, if any, you attach to my opinion but it might interest you to know that to one rather snooty reader, at least, it seems about the best comic book ever written by an American. It is simply devastating to about seven-eighths of the work of imitation Andersons, to facile and "correct" culture and to this eternal looking beyond appearances for the "real," on the part of people who have never even been conscious of appearances. The thing is like a nightmare of literary preten-

sions behind which a certain hilarious order establishes itself before the end—so it hasn't that quality of leaving a painful passionate *funnyness* as the last taste in your mouth. Like Alice in Wonderland it sends you back to the sane world above cant and fashion in which most of us flatter ourselves that we live—sometimes.

Beyond that it is absorbingly interesting—the failure to be that is the one unforgivable sin. Frankly I hope you won't like it—because I am something of a ballyhoo man for Scribners and I'd some day like to see all my generation (3) that I admire rounded up in the same coop—but knowing my entheusiasm and his own trepidation Ernest agreed with me that such a statement of the former might break the ice for what is an extraordinary and unusual production.

With Best Wishes to you Both
Your Friend
      F. Scott Fitzg—

Hemingway submitted *Torrents* to Liveright on 7 December with a cover letter mentioning Fitzgerald's high opinion of the work. Fitzgerald appears in *Torrents* in a ponderously facetious "Author's Note to the Reader":

It was at this point in the story, reader, that Mr. F. Scott Fitzgerald came to our home one afternoon, and after remaining for quite a while suddenly sat down in the fireplace and would not (or was it could not, reader?) get up and let the fire burn something else so as to keep the room warm. I know, reader, that these things sometimes do not show in a story, but, just the same, they are happening, and think what they mean to chaps like you and me in the literary game. If you should think this part of the story is not as good as it might have been remember, reader, that day in and day out all over the world things like this are happening. Need I add, reader, that I have the utmost respect for Mr. Fitzgerald, and let anyone else attack him and I would be the first to spring to his defense! And that includes you, too, reader, though I hate to speak out bluntly like this, and take the risk of breaking up a friendship of the sort that ours has gotten to be.

Fitzgerald's response to this passage is not known; but he was probably not greatly amused, for it shows him as helplessly drunk. Although Fitzgerald at that time cultivated his reputation as a drinker, he resisted being classified as a drunk—an image which he felt would injure the serious reception of his novels. Whatever Hemingway intended in his treatment of Fitzgerald in *Torrents,* it should have served as a warning. The next time Hemingway used Fitzgerald in print—in "The Snows of Kilimanjaro"—the effect would be unequivocal. Hemingway presented the carbon-copy typescript of *Torrents* to the Fitzgeralds, inscribed "To Scott and Zelda with love from Ernest."

On 15 December 1925, Hemingway sent Fitzgerald from Schruns in the Austrian alps a little treatise on *Subject,* stating that war is the best subject for fiction because it provides so much material that is otherwise unavailable. Nonetheless, he consoles Scott for having missed the war, admitting that he himself did not get any worth while material out of the war—except personally— because he was too young. Other good subjects are love, money, avarice, and murder. He cites impotence as a dull subject—his private joke, since that was a subject of *The Sun Also Rises.*

Horace Liveright declined *The Torrents of Spring* by cable and wrote Hemingway on 30 December 1925: ". . . who on earth do you think would buy it? Apart from the fact it is a bitter, and I might say vicious caricature of Sherwood Anderson, it is entirely cerebral. . . . We disagree with you and Scott Fitzgerald and Louis Bromfield and Dos Passos that it is a fine American Satire." Liveright wanted to see Hemingway's novel. At this point, Fitzgerald became actively involved as Hemingway's agent with Perkins, although it is impossible to determine how much authority he really had in the matter. At the end of December Fitzgerald sent Perkins a confidential report on the status of *Torrents:*

> (2) Hemmingways book (not his novel) is a 28,000 word satire on Sherwood Anderson and his imitators called The *Torrents of Spring.* I loved it, but believe it wouldn't be popular, + Liveright have refused it—*they are backing Anderson* and the book is almost a vicious parody on him. You see I agree with Ernest that Anderson's last two books have let every-

THE TORRENTS OF SPRING

A Romantic Novel In Honor of The Passing Of
A Great Race.

By ERNEST HEMINGWAY.

*To Scott and Zelda
with love from Ernest.*

And perhaps there is one reason why a
comic writer should of all others be
the least excused for deviating from
nature, since it may not be always
so easy for a serious poet to meet with
the great and the admirable; but life
everywhere furnishes an accurate observ-
er with the ridiculous.

Henry Fielding.

F. Scott Fitzgerald Papers, Princeton University Library

body down who believed in him—I think they're cheap, faked, obscurantic and awful. Hemmingway thinks, but isn't yet sure to my satisfaction, that their refusal sets him free from his three book (letter) agreement with them. In that case I think he'll give you his novel (on condition you'll publish satire first—probable sale 1000 copies) which he is now revising in Austria. Harcourt has just written Louie Bromfield that to get the novel they'll publish satire, sight unseen (utterly confidential) and Knopf is after him via Aspinwall Bradley.

He and I are very thick + he's marking time until he finds out how much he's bound to Liveright. If he's free I'm *almost* sure I can get satire to you first + then if you see your way clear you can contract for the novel *tout ensemble*. He's anxious too to get a foothold in your magazine—one story I've sent you— the other, to my horror he'd given for about $40 to an "arty" publication called *This Quarter,* over here.

He's *dead set* on having the satire published first. His idea has always been to come to you + his only hesitation has been that Harcourt might be less conservative in regard to certain somewhat broad scenes. His adress is:

Herr Ernest Hemmingway
Hotel Taube   Don't even tell him I've dis-
Schrunns   cussed his Liveright + Har-
Vorarlburg   court relations with you.
Austria

As soon as he has definate dope I'll pass it on to you I wanted a strong wire to show you were as interested, and more, than Harcourt. Did you know your letter just missed by two weeks getting *In Our Time.* It had no sale of course but I think the novel may be something extraordinary—Tom Boyd and E. E. Cummings + Biggs combined.

Since Fitzgerald warns Perkins not to let Hemingway know how much he has revealed in this letter, it seems that his role in bringing Hemingway to Scribners was at least partly self-delegated. It is clear that Hemingway did seek Fitzgerald's advice. On 31 December he reported to Fitzgerald from Schruns on his negotiations with Boni & Liveright, Knopf, and Harcourt, Brace. Although Alfred Harcourt is eager to sign him up, Ernest is willing to risk losing the

Paris, Christmas 1925.

contract in order to become a Scribners author because of his respect for Perkins and because he would like to be published with Scott. Ernest asks him to write Perkins preparing the way for *The Torrents of Spring.* He is relying on Scott in this matter and asks whether he should go to America to see Perkins. Fitzgerald cabled Perkins on 8 January 1926: YOU CAN GET HEMINGWAYS FINISHED NOVEL PROVIDED YOU PUBLISH UNPROMISING SATIRE HARCOURT HAS MADE DEFINITE OFFER WIRE IMMEDIATELY WITHOUT QUALIFICATIONS. Perkins responded the same day: PUBLISH NOVEL AT FIFTEEN PERCENT AND ADVANCE IF DESIRED ALSO SATIRE UNLESS OBJECTIONABLE OTHER THAN FINANCIALLY. On the 11th Perkins cabled Fitzgerald again: CONFIDENCE ABSOLUTE KEEN TO PUBLISH HIM.

Perkins was ready to accept Hemingway's novel and an uncommercial satire sight unseen, largely on his trust in Fitzgerald's enthusiasm. Fitzgerald had not read the novel. Although Hemingway had a complete draft of *The Sun Also Rises,* he would not let Fitzgerald read it. "CONFIDENCE ABSOLUTE" expressed Perkins' confidence in Fitzgerald's instinct as well as his confidence in Hemingway's future.

On 13 January 1926 Perkins wrote Fitzgerald detailing his position:

> I did my best with that cable, but there was a fear that this satire—although in the hands of such a writer it could hardly be rightly so upon any theory—might be suppressible. . . . But I believe that as compared with most others [publishers], Hemingway would be better off in our hands because we are absolutely true to our authors and support them loyally in the face of losses for a long time, when we believe in their qualities and in them. It is that kind of a publisher that Hemingway probably needs, because I hardly think he could come into a large public immediately.

Early in 1926 Hemingway wrote from Schruns responding to Fitzgerald's ranking of the *In Our Time* stories. Hemingway assigns grade I to "Big Two-Hearted River," "Indian Camp," "Soldier's Home" and to first and last paragraphs of "Out of Season." "Cat in the Rain"—a story about a young wife who wants a home married to a man who doesn't want to be tied down by domesticity —was not about Hadley Hemingway, although Scott and Zelda thought it was. The story was based on a young couple Ernest met while covering the Genoa conference. Hadley did figure in "Out of Season," which is virtually a report of what happened. Ernest says that his ear is sharper after an argument, and that he wrote the story directly on the typewriter after the bad fishing trip that produced the story. The drunken guide hanged himself after Ernest reported him, but he had left that out because he wanted to write a story that would be tragic without violence.

This six-page holograph letter goes on to discuss Hemingway's attitude toward two Paris figures, Harold Stearns and Robert Mc-

Almon. Stearns—who would appear in *The Sun Also Rises* as Harvey Stone—was a promising American writer who had gone to alcoholic seed in Paris. Fitzgerald was trying to help him, but Hemingway advises that nothing can be done about Stearns and that Scott should not give him any more money. McAlmon was an American expatriate writer who was better known as the publisher of the Paris-based Contact Editions. Upon his marriage to the English writer Bryher, McAlmon received a gift of money from her father, Sir John Ellerman. Much of it went into the Contact Editions, which published McAlmon's work and that of other writers as well. McAlmon was capable of great generosity to other writers but was also a trouble-making gossiper. As his own work failed to achieve recognition, he became resentful of Hemingway's success. McAlmon had been Hemingway's first publisher when Contact brought out *Three Stories & Ten Poems* in 1923; and McAlmon may also have participated in the publication of *in our time,* which was jointly dedicated to McAlmon and William Bird.

Ernest reports to Scott that after he called McAlmon on something he said about Scott, McAlmon began accusing him of ingratitude, although Ernest doesn't think that McAlmon did much for him. Ernest notes that he didn't get anything for the "books" McAlmon published. (This was a weak position, for there was little to be made from 300 copies of a $2 publication—at 10 percent royalty, a maximum of $60. McAlmon gave Hemingway his first book publication, which greatly aided his career at a time when his stories were unplaceable.) Hemingway plans to retaliate by writing a story ridiculing McAlmon. The story was not written, but his feud with McAlmon became increasingly nasty and involved Fitzgerald. Someone less impressed with Hemingway than Fitzgerald was might have begun to feel a certain uneasiness at the developing record of his feuds. Ernest is getting two illustrated German war books for Scott. He is re-reading the eighteenth-century Navy novels of Frederick Marryat and recommends four: *Peter Simple, Frank Mildmay, Mr. Midshipman Easy,* and *Snarleyyow or, the Dog Fiend.* He is delighted by the discovery that Ostereich means The Eastern Kingdom and asks Scott to tell Zelda.

While Hemingway was making plans to go to New York from Schruns, Fitzgerald prepared the way for him, writing to Perkins in January from Salies-de-Béarn in the Pyrenees, where Zelda Fitzgerald was taking a cure for colitis: "To hear him talk you'd think Liveright had broken up his home and robbed him of millions—but thats because he knows nothing of publishing, except in the cucoo magazines, is very young and feels helpless so far away. You won't be able to help liking him—he's one of the nicest fellows I ever knew."

Hemingway arrived in New York aboard the *Mauretania* on 9 February. His first call was at Boni & Liveright, where he and Horace Liveright agreed to terminate their contract. The next day Hemingway called on Perkins. By this time Perkins had almost certainly read *The Torrents of Spring,* for Donald Ogden Stewart had recovered the typescript from Boni & Liveright and delivered it to Scribners. Hemingway brought the first draft of *The Sun Also Rises* to New York, but there is no evidence that Perkins read it at this meeting. Perkins offered a $1500 advance on the parody and the novel against a 15 percent royalty. These terms were generous for a literary parody and a first novel. Perkins obviously liked *Torrents,* but it was certainly not commercial. The property was Ernest Hemingway, and Perkins—a brilliant talent prospector—was betting on him.

Perkins and Hemingway impressed each other. Perkins was forty-one. After graduating from Harvard, he had joined Scribners in 1910. From old New England stock, Perkins was personally reserved and conservative. Nonetheless, he was responsible for shifting the Scribners image from an old-line, traditional publisher to a publisher of the best new writers. His first major literary find had been F. Scott Fitzgerald, and his authors eventually included Ring Lardner, Ernest Hemingway, and Thomas Wolfe. His relationships with his authors were close. Perkins was attracted to Hemingway by more than a recognition of talent, for he enjoyed masculine company. The father of five daughters, Perkins longed for a son. It has been said that his authors became surrogate sons. Nonetheless, Perkins was sometimes embarrassed by Hemingway. A favorite anecdote in American publishing involves Perkins' inability to speak the obscenities he was trying to persuade Hemingway to omit from his writing. On one such occasion Hemingway got him to write the word "fuck" on his desk calendar. Later, while

Maxwell Perkins.

Perkins was out of the office, Charles Scribner came looking for him and was surprised to find the calendar notation. One version of the anecdote has it that when Perkins returned to the office, Scribner solicitously asked, "Don't you want to take the rest of the day off, Max? You must be exhausted."

Hemingway was in New York when Scribners published *All the Sad Young Men,* Fitzgerald's third story collection, on 26 February. It was a strong volume, including "The Rich Boy" novelette, "Winter Dreams," "Absolution," and " 'The Sensible Thing.' " The first printing of 10,000 copies sold rapidly, and two more printings of 3000 each were required.

Fitzgerald was out of touch in the Pyrenees. On about 1 March —after Hemingway had left New York—he sent Perkins more advice on dealing with Hemingway, delicately indicating that his ethics were shaky: "In any case he is temperamental in business. made so by these bogus publishers over here. If you take the other two things *get a signed contract* for The *Sun Also Rises* (novel) Anyhow this is my last word on the subject—confidential between you + me. Please destroy this letter." The "other two things" refers to *Torrents* and the short story "Fifty Grand" Fitzgerald had urged Hemingway to submit to *Scribner's Magazine*. Perkins asked Hemingway to cut the story for space reasons, not content. Hemingway was not able to cut it, but accepted the offer by the writer Manuel Komroff to cut it for him. Komroff's editing was unsatisfactory, and the story did not appear until *The Atlantic Monthly* published it in July 1927. "Fifty Grand" triggered a permanent resentment against Fitzgerald in Hemingway because Fitzgerald had persuaded him to delete the anecdote about Jack Brennan's fight with Benny Leonard which opened the story, because it was too well known.[4] When asked how he was able to beat Leonard, Brennan replies that Benny is a very smart boxer who is always thinking in the ring; all the time Benny was thinking, Brennan was hitting

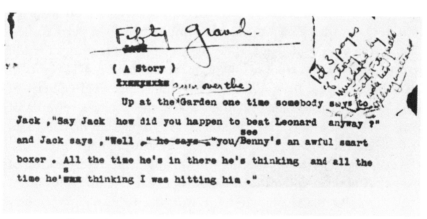

Ernest Hemingway Collection, John F. Kennedy Library.

4 Hemingway's character Jack Brennan was based on Jack Britton, welterweight champion from 1919 to 1922. Benny Leonard was lightweight champion from 1917 to 1924. Britton beat Leonard on a foul in 1922.

him. Hemingway regarded this comment as an important piece of boxing metaphysics and came to feel that it had been a mistake to accept Fitzgerald's advice. In one of the typescripts of "Fifty Grand" that he saved, Hemingway noted: "1st 3 pages of story mutilated by Scott Fitzgerald with his [undecipherable]." When he wrote an unpublished essay, "The Art of the Short Story and Nine Stories to Prove It" in 1959, Hemingway blamed his acceptance of Fitzgerald's bad advice on his own "humility." Nevertheless, he acknowledged that Fitzgerald was more concerned about Hemingway's career than his own.

In the first week of March 1926 Hemingway stopped off in Paris on his way back to Schruns and reported to Fitzgerald on his meeting with Perkins—as well as on the play version of *The Great Gatsby*, which he had seen on Broadway. Hemingway's real reason for being in Paris was to see Pauline Pfeiffer, the Arkansas heiress with whom he was having a clandestine affair. He would write bitterly and guiltily about this affair in *A Moveable Feast*. From all accounts it is clear that Pauline moved in relentlessly on the Hemingway marriage, establishing herself as Hadley's close friend and welcome guest on the Hemingways' trips. Pauline urged Hemingway to publish *The Torrents of Spring*, against Hadley's advice.

While Hemingway was rewriting *The Sun Also Rises* in winter–spring 1926 Fitzgerald was having trouble getting on with his own work. In 1926 he wrote only two undistinguished short stories, "Your Way and Mine" and "The Dance," but his earnings for the year topped $25,000 from his share of the play and movie rights to *The Great Gatsby*. In his *Ledger* Fitzgerald reprovingly described 1925–26 as "Futile, shameful useless but the $30,000 rewards of 1924 work. Self disgust. Health gone." He knew what he had to do at this point in his career: consolidate the achievement of *Gatsby*. His plan was to write an ambitious novel about the deterioration of a young American under the influence of expatriate life. This novel was to involve matricide; and the working titles were variously "Our Type," "The World's Fair," "The Melarky Case," and "The Boy Who Killed His Mother." The murder material developed from his interest in the Dorothy Ellingson matricide case of 1925 and the sensational Leopold-Loeb case of 1924. He worked on the matricide plot with many interruptions from 1925 to 1930, accumulating five incomplete drafts.

The plot of the novel can be reconstructed from the drafts. Francis Melarky (the name indicates Fitzgerald's identification with the character and his reservations about the material) is a twenty-one-year-old Southerner touring Europe, against his will, with his mother. The narrative opens with their arrival on the Riviera, at which point Francis has been beaten by the police in consequence of a drunken brawl in Rome. Before coming to Europe he had been dismissed from West Point and had then worked as a technician in Hollywood, where he had been involved with an actress. Francis has a quick and violent temper which his mother triggers by reminding him of his failures. Her attempts to control Francis have alienated him, so that she employs deceit. On the Riviera Francis is taken up by an attractive group of Americans led by Seth and Dinah Roreback (or Piper), which includes Abe Herkimer, an alcoholic composer. Francis attempts to obtain work at an American movie studio on the Riviera, but his plans are sabotaged by his mother, who regards movie people as a bad influence on him. With nothing better to do, he accepts the Rorebacks' invitation to go to Paris. In Paris Francis falls in love with Dinah, who is flattered but does not develop any romantic feelings for him. The manuscripts break off at this point, but other sources indicate that Francis would suffer a breakdown—probably from drinking—and murder his mother in a fit of rage. The ways in which these drafts evolved into *Tender Is the Night* (1934) are clear, as Fitzgerald salvaged the characters and setting while abandoning the matricide material. Francis Melarky became Rosemary Hoyt; the Rorebacks became the Divers; Abe Herkimer became Abe North. The plot of *Tender Is the Night* concerns a psychiatrist who is ruined by his marriage to a wealthy former mental patient; this material drew upon Zelda Fitzgerald's mental breakdown in 1930.

Fitzgerald discussed the plot and material of his new novel with Hemingway. In April 1926 Hemingway wrote from Paris to Fitzgerald on the Riviera announcing the completion of *The Sun Also Rises* rewrite—which he doesn't think Scott will like—including a burlesque of Fitzgerald's work-in-progress:

[41]

I have tried to follow the outline and spirit of the Great Gatsby but I feel I have failed somewhat because of never having been on Long Island. The hero, like Gatsby, is a Lake Superior Salmon Fisherman. (There are no salmon in Lake Superior) The action all takes place in Newport, R.I. and the heroine is a girl named Sophie Irene Loeb who kills her mother. The scene in which Sophie gives birth to twins in the death house at Sing Sing where she is waiting to be electrocuted for the murder of the father and sister of her, as then, unborn children I got from Dreiser but practically everything else in the book is either my own or yours. I know you'll be glad to see it. The Sun Also Rises comes from Sophie's statement as she is strapped into the chair as the current mounts.

Ernest plans to dedicate the novel to his son, with the line "This Collection of Instructive Anecdotes." In case that worries Scott, *The Sun Also Rises* is not anecdotal— nor does it resemble Dos Passos' *Manhattan Transfer* or Anderson's *Dark Laughter*. He expresses his anger at Ernest Walsh, editor of *This Quarter,* who has attacked him in a poem; analyzes the aesthetic and psychological shortcomings of Fitzgerald's close friend Ring Lardner; and urges him to write his novel with the ancillary income from *The Great Gatsby*. Ernest lists various gag benefactions he has arranged to help with Scott's finances: Pauline Pfeiffer will give Scott her job on *Vogue,* and Ernest has arranged for all of his royalties to go to Scott. Ernest has not seen Scott's article on him in *The Bookman* but thanks him for "services rendered." He will bring the revised typescript of *The Sun Also Rises* to the Riviera and welcomes Scott's advice on it. The six-page letter is signed "Herbert J. Horseshit."

Hemingway regarded Fitzgerald's financial problems as absurd, and on the 24th of April he wrote to Perkins repeating the joke about donating his royalties to Scott. Hemingway's future royalties were problematical. *The Torrents of Spring,* published on 28 May 1926 in a printing of 1250 copies, sold slowly. It did provide a launching platform for *The Sun Also Rises,* for it was widely reviewed. Allen Tate's review in *The Nation* called Hemingway "the best contemporary writer of eighteenth-century prose" and hailed *Torrents* as "the most economically realized humor of disproportion that this reviewer has read in American prose." Tate was a friend of Hemingway's at that time.

On the 4th of May, Hemingway wrote to Fitzgerald to say he missed him and wanted to talk to him. Later in the month Hemingway wrote from Madrid—in reply to a lost letter from Fitzgerald—apologizing for his April letter that seemed to dismiss Scott's *Bookman* article. He explains that he was merely agreeing with Scott's position that reviews didn't help the writer unless they were favorable and promoted sales. The only instructional material in *The Sun Also Rises* is about "how people go to hell"; but if it worries Scott, Ernest will delete that line from the dedication. He admits that Scott is right about Ring Lardner. This letter is signed "Ernest M. Shit."

Glenway Wescott recalls that in the summer of 1925 or 1926 Fitzgerald tried to persuade him to help launch Hemingway. Wescott—who would be travestied in *The Sun Also Rises* as Robert Prentiss—was impressed by Fitzgerald's naive assumption that he shared the desire to aid a rival writer. Fitzgerald believed that Hemingway was "inimitably, essentially superior." Wescott became convinced that Fitzgerald's admiration for Hemingway culminated in the feeling that he could abandon his literary responsibilities to Hemingway. This view can certainly be challenged, for it discounts Fitzgerald's considerable appetite for fame and even immortality. Nonetheless, Wescott's testimony indicates the intensity of Fitzgerald's commitment to Hemingway's career.

Fitzgerald did not read the typescript of *The Sun Also Rises* until June 1926, when the Hemingways (who were joined by Pauline Pfeiffer) came to the Riviera. The Fitzgeralds had rented the Villa Paquita at Juan-les-Pins, but it did not suit them, and they turned it over to the Hemingways.

The Fitzgeralds' closest friends at that time were Gerald and Sara Murphy, wealthy American expatriates who devoted themselves to living well. The Murphys were not frivolous people, for Gerald was seriously interested in painting and literature. His paintings have been recognized as precursors of the Pop-Art school; and the Murphys' friends included John Dos Passos, Archibald MacLeish, and Philip Barry. Fitzgerald had introduced Hemingway to the Murphys in 1925, and Gerald became one of his strongest admirers. The Hemingway-Murphy relationship was close for more than a decade. Late in his life Hemingway became convinced that the Murphys had corrupted him with their praise and had encouraged the dissolution of his marriage with Hadley. In *A Moveable Feast* he arraigned them as "the rich" who, aided by their "pilot fish" John Dos Passos, had violated his innocence.

When Hemingway arrived at Juan-les-Pins in early June 1926 the Murphys gave a champagne party at the Casino to welcome him. Fitzgerald resented this party and spoiled it with his drunken antics. After Fitzgerald began tossing ashtrays at tables, Murphy left his own party. This summer was supposed to be devoted to hard work and sobriety, but Fitzgerald continued to drink steadily and made no progress with his novel. Zelda Fitzgerald remarked that the novel "goes so slow it ought to be serialized in the Encyclopedia Britannica."

In *A Moveable Feast* Hemingway states, "Scott did not see it [*The Sun Also Rises*] until after the completely rewritten and cut manuscript had been sent to Scribners at the end of April." This statement is true; but the implication that Hemingway did not avail himself of Fitzgerald's editorial judgment is misleading. Fitzgerald read a carbon copy in early June while proof was being set in New York. His ten-page critique—which Hemingway preserved—establishes that Hemingway acted on Fitzgerald's recommendations in galley proof.

Dear Ernest: Nowdays when almost everyone is a genius, at least for awhile, the temptation for the bogus to profit is no greater than the temptation for the good man to relax (in one mysterious way or another)—not realizing the transitory quality of his glory because he forgets that it rests on the frail shoulders of professional enthusiasts. This should frighten all of us into a lust for anything honest that people have to say about our work. I've taken what proved to be excellent advice (On The B. + Damned) from Bunny Wilson who never wrote a novel, (on Gatsby —change of many thousand wds) from Max Perkins who never considered writing one, and on T. S. of Paradise from Katherine Tighe (you don't know her) who had probably never read a novel before.

[This is beginning to sound like my own current work which resolves itself into laborious + sententious preliminaries].

Anyhow I think parts of *Sun Also* are careless + ineffectual. As I said yestiday (and, as I recollect, in trying to get you to cut the 1st part of 50 Grand) I find in you the same tendency to envelope or (and as it usually turns out) to *embalm* in mere wordiness an anecdote or joke thats casually appealed to you, that I find in myself in trying to preserve a piece of "fine writing." Your first chapter contains about 10 such things and it gives a feeling of condescending *casuallness.*

P.1. "highly moral story"
"Brett said" (O.Henry stuff)
"much too expensive"

"something or other" (if you don't want to tell, why waste 3 wds. saying it. See P.23—"*9 or 14*" and "or how many years it was since 19XX" when it would take two words to say That's what youd kid in anyone else as mere "style"—mere horseshit I can't find this latter but anyhow you've not only got to write well yourself but you've also got to not-do what anyone can do and I think that there are about 24 sneers, superiorities, and nose-thumbings-at-nothing that mar the whole narrative up to p. 29 where (after a false start on the introduction of Cohn) it really gets going. And to preserve these perverse and willfull non-essentials you've done a lot of writing that *honestly* reminded me of Michael Arlen.

[You know the very fact that people have committed themselves to you will make them watch you like a cat. + if they don't like it creap away like one]

For example.

Pps. 1+2. Snobbish (not in itself but because the history of English Aristocrats in the war, set down so verbosely so uncritically, so exteriorly and yet so obviously inspired from within, is *shopworn*.) You had the same problem that I had with my Rich Boy, previously debauched by Chambers ect. Either bring more thot to it with the realization that that ground has already raised its wheat + weeds or cut it down to seven sentences. It hasn't even your rythym and the fact that may be "true" is utterly immaterial.

That biography from you, who allways believed in the superiority (the preferability) of the *imagined* to the *seen not to say to the merely recounted*.

P.3.   "Beautifully engraved shares" (Beautifully engraved 1886 irony) All this is O.K. but so glib *when* its glib + *so* profuse.

P.5.   Painters are no longer *real* in prose. They must be minimized. [This is not done by making them schlptors, backhouse wall-experts or miniature painters]

P.8.   "highly moral urges" "because I believe its a good story" If this paragraph isn't maladroit then I'm a rewrite man for Dr. Cadman.

P.9.   Somehow its not good. I can't quite put my hand on it—it has a ring of "This is a true story ect."

P.10.   "Quarter being a state of mind ect." This is an all guide books. I havn't read Basil Swoon's but I have fifty francs to lose.

[About this time I can hear you say "Jesus this guy thinks I'm lousy, + he can stick it up his ass for all I give a Gd Dm for his 'critisism'." But remember this is a new departure for you, and that I think your stuff is great. You were the first American I wanted to meet in Europe —and the last. (This latter clause is simply to balance the sentence. It doesn't seem to make sense tho I have pawed at it for several minutes. Its like the age of the French women.)

P.14.   (+ thereabout) as I said yesterday I think this anecdote is flat as hell without naming Ford which would be cheap.

It's flat because you end with mention of Allister Crowly. If he's nobody its nothing. If he's somebody, its cheap. This is a novel. Also I'd cut out mention of H. Stearns earlier.

———————————————

Why not cut the inessentials in Cohens biography?

[46]

His first marriage is of no importance. When so many people can write well + the competition is so heavy I can't imagine how you could have done these first 20 pps. so casually. You can't *play* with peoples attention—a good man who has the power of arresting attention at will must be especially careful.

From here Or rather from p. 30 I began to like the novel but Ernest I can't tell you the sense of disappointment that beginning with its elephantine facetiousness gave me. Please do what you can about it in proof. Its 7500 words—you could reduce it to 5000. And my advice is not to do it by mere pareing but to take out the worst of the *scenes.*

I've decided not to pick at anything else, because I wasn't at all inspired to pick when reading it. I was much too excited. Besides This is probably a heavy dose. The novel's damn good. The centrol theme is marred somewhere but hell! unless you're writing your life history where you have an inevitable pendulum to swing you true (Harding metaphor), who can bring it entirely off? And what critic can trace whether the fault lies in a possible insufficient thinking out, in the biteing off of more than you eventually cared to chew in the impotent theme or in the elusiveness of the lady character herself. My theory always was that she dramatized herself in terms of Arlen's dramatatization of somebody's dramatizatatg of Stephen McKenna's dramatization of Diana Manner's dramatization of the last girl in Well's *Tono Bungay*—who's original probably liked more things about Beatrix Esmond than about Jane Austin's Elizabeth (to whom we owe the manners of so many of our wives.)

Appropos of your foreward about the Latin quarter —suppose you had begun your stories with phrases like: "Spain is a peculiar place—ect" or "Michigan is interesting to two classes—the fisherman + the drummer."

Pps 64 + 65 with a bit of work should tell all that need be known about *Brett's* past.
(Small point) "Dysemtry" instead of "killed" is a clichês to avoid a cliché. It stands out. I suppose it can't be helped. I suppose all the 75,000000 Europeans who died between

1914-1918 will always be among the 10,000,000 who were killed in the war.

God! The bottom of p. 77 Jusque the top p. 78 are wonderful, I go crazy when people aren't always at their best. This isn't picked out—I just happened on it.

The heart of my critisim beats somewhere apon p. 87. I think you can't change it, though. I felt the lack of some crazy torturing tentativeness or security—horror, all at once, that she'd feel—and he'd feel—maybe I'm crazy. He isn't *like an impotent man. He's like a man in a sort of moral chastity belt.*

Oh, well. It's fine, from Chap V on, anyhow, in spite of that—which fact is merely a proof of its brilliance.

Station Z.W.X. square says good night. Good night all.

In the typescript and galley proof of *The Sun Also Rises* Chapter I recounts Brett Ashley's marital history and provides background on her liaison with Mike Campbell. Chapter II describes Jake's life in Paris, his newspaper job, and his dislike of the Quarter. Robert Cohn's novel is discussed. Braddocks got Jake to read it so he wouldn't have to read it himself. Mention of Braddocks (who was Ford Madox Ford) sets up the anecdote about Braddocks cutting Aleister Crowley at the Closerie de Lilas—which was salvaged thirty years later in *A Moveable Feast.* Jake explains to the reader that it is necessary to include Braddocks because he is Cohn's friend, and that Cohn is the hero of the novel. Then at the end of galley 3 appear the opening words of the published novel: "Robert Cohn was once middleweight boxing champion of Princeton."

Hemingway acted on Fitzgerald's urging to cut the opening expository material, although *A Moveable Feast* conveys the impression that he regarded Fitzgerald's editorial advice as worthless. Fitzgerald's other major criticism (p. 87—the scene in Chapter VII when Brett comes to Jake's flat) was that Hemingway had not conveyed Jake's feelings about his impotence adequately, a serious reservation in the case of a character who has lost his penis. The section that Fitzgerald singled out for praise ("God! The bottom of

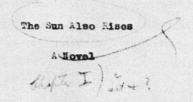

The Sun Also Rises

A Novel

Chapter I 2d+?

    This is a novel about a lady. Her name is Lady
Ashley and when the story begins she is living in Paris
and it is Spring. That should be a good setting for a
romantic but highly moral story. As every one knows Paris
is a very romantic place. Spring in Paris is a very happy
and romantic time. Autumn in Paris, although very beautiful,
might give a note of sadness or melancholy that we shall
try to keep out of this story.
    Lady Ashley was born Elizabeth Brett Murray.
Her title came from her second husband. She had divorced
one husband for something or other, mutual consent; not
until after he had put one of those notices in the papers
stating that after this date he would not be responsible
for any debt, etc. He was a Scotchman and found Brett
much too expensive, especially as she had only married him
to get rid of him and to get away from home. At present
she had a legal separation from her second husband, who
had the title, because he was a dipsomaniac, he having
learned it in the North Sea commanding a mine-sweeper,
Brett said. When he had gotten to be a proper thorough
going dipsomaniac and found that Brett did not love him he

Sale Number 3966 Important Modern First Editions . . . Sotheby Parke Bernet
(1977), #154.

p. 77 Jusque the top of p. 78 are wonderful") is the scene in Chapter
VI where Frances Clyne berates Cohn for discarding her.

    It is not strange that Fitzgerald would have written a ten-page
memo to a man he was seeing daily. As the preamble shows, he was
aware that he was taking a risk in criticizing the novel at all. Hemingway never responded mildly to criticism, and Fitzgerald was obviously concerned about alienating his greatly admired friend. A

document was required to prepare for discussion of the novel. There were extended talks, in which Hemingway was persuaded to cut the opening of *The Sun Also Rises*. On 5 June 1926 Hemingway informed Perkins that Fitzgerald is reading the novel and agrees with Hemingway that the first chapters should be cut. Fitzgerald did not report to Perkins until about 25 June because of a trip to Paris to have Zelda's appendix removed:

> First as to Ernests book. I liked it but with certain qualifications. The fiesta, the fishing trip, the minor characters were fine. The lady I didn't like, perhaps because I don't like the original. In the mutilated man I thought Ernest bit off more than can yet be chewn between the covers of a book, then lost his nerve a little and edited the more vitalizing details out. He has since told me that something like this happened. Do ask him for the absolute minimum of nessessary changes, Max— he's so discouraged about the previous reception of his work by publishers and magazine editors. (Tho he loved your letter) From the latter he has had a lot of words and until Bridges offer for the short story ["Fifty Grand"] (from which he had even before cut out a thousand words on my recommendation) scarcely a single dollar. From the *Torrents* I expect you'll have little response. Do you think the Bookman article did him any good?

Zelda Fitzgerald also read the typescript of *The Sun Also Rises* and was far less impressed with it than her husband was. Sara Mayfield, a girlhood friend from Montgomery, visited the Fitzgeralds on the Riviera that summer. When asked what Hemingway's novel was about, Zelda replied that it was about "Bullfighting, bullslinging, and bull. . . ." Fitzgerald cut Zelda off, telling her not to talk that way about Hemingway. Miss Mayfield reports in her book about the Fitzgeralds, *Exiles from Paradise,* that Zelda was disturbed by Hemingway's influence on Fitzgerald. She blamed Hemingway for encouraging the drinking bouts that interrupted Fitzgerald's work and was repelled by Hemingway's "morbid preoccupation with offbeat sex and the sadism and necrophilia that go with it." Sara Mayfield's book has an affectionate portrayal of Zelda; nonetheless, it is noteworthy that Zelda Fitzgerald and Hemingway made the same charges against each other's influence on Fitzgerald's working habits.

The Fitzgeralds did not join the Hemingways, Pauline Pfeiffer, and the Murphys on their early July trip to the Fiesta of San Fermín at Pamplona. There is no evidence that the Fitzgeralds were invited along; but if they were, Zelda's appendectomy prevented them from going. Fitzgerald never attended a bullfight with Hemingway. After Pamplona the Hemingways returned to the Riviera for the rest of July and August.

Having succeeded in bringing Hemingway to Scribners, Fitzgerald then planned to have Hemingway represented by his agent, Harold Ober, who was with the Paul Revere Reynolds agency and handled Fitzgerald's magazine material. Fitzgerald hoped that Ober would be able to sell Hemingway's stories to the American magazines. Until 1927 all of Hemingway's short stories were published by little magazines, which made little more than token payments. Short stories provided the basis of Fitzgerald's income, and he felt that Hemingway should also be receiving good money—as well as American visibility—for his stories. In the summer and fall of 1926 Fitzgerald unsuccessfully attempted to set up a connection between Ober and Hemingway. The reasons why this arrangement fell through are not entirely clear. Part of the problem was that Paul Revere Reynolds, Ober's partner, apparently tried to represent Hemingway without consulting Ober. It is possible that Hemingway was suspicious about having an agent. He never employed one, except for the sale of movie rights.

In late August or September of 1926, after Hemingway had returned to Paris, Fitzgerald wrote to say that he was hard at work on his novel. This claim would become a refrain over the next years as Fitzgerald attempted to convince Hemingway that he was truly a serious writer—and as Hemingway tried to encourage him to stick with the novel.

Dear Ernest:

Sorry we missed you + Hadley. No news. I'm on the wagon + working like hell. Expect to sail for N.Y December 10th from Genoa on the *Conte Biancamo.* Will be here till then. Saw Bullfight in Frejus. Bull was euneuch

[51]

(sp.). House barred + dark. Front door chained. Have made no enemies for a week. Hamilton domestic row ended in riot. Have new war books by Pierrefeu. God is love.

Signed
Ernestine Murphy.

Did you read in the N.Y Herald about—
"... Henry Carpenter, banker, and Willie Stevens, half-wit, ..."

Fitzgerald's note was written on the bottom of a letter from Harold Ober reporting his inability to place "Fifty Grand" and asking for other Hemingway stories.

While awaiting publication of *The Sun Also Rises* Hemingway wrote to Fitzgerald from Paris in September that he and Hadley have separated, admitting that it is his fault. Ernest has cut the first part of the novel to start with Cohn and has done considerable rewriting in proof. He hopes Scott will like it now and thinks he will. Ernest plans to come to Marseilles to see Scott soon. Ernest Walsh—editor of *This Quarter*—is now attacking Hemingway for selling out to Scribners.

Like many others, Fitzgerald—who was puritanical when sober—felt compelled to emulate Hemingway's bawdy humor. His September reply to Hemingway's letter included a scatological parody of the *In Our Time* vignettes.

We were in a back-house in Juan-les-Pins. Bill had lost controll of his splincter muscles. There were wet *Matins* in the rack beside the door. There were wet *Eclairers de Nice* in the rack over his head. When the King of Bulgeria came in Bill was just firing a burst that struck the old limeshit twenty feet down with a *splat-tap*. All the rest came just like that. The King of Bulgaria began to whirl round and round.

"The great thing in these affairs—" he said.

Soon he was whirling faster and faster. Then he was dead.

At this point in my letter my 30th birthday came and

I got tight for a week in the company of such facinating gents as Mr. Theodore Rousseau + other ornaments of what is now a barren shore.

Ernest of little faith I hope the sale of The Killers will teach you to send every story either to Scribners or an agent. Can't you get "Today is Friday" back? Your letter depressed and rather baffled me. Have you and Hadley permanently busted up, and was the nessessity of that what was on your soul this summer. Don't answer this unless you feel like it. Anyhow I'm sorry everything's such a mess and I do want to see you if you come to Marseitte in October.

We saw the Murphys before they left, got stewed with them (at their party)—that is we got stewed—and I believe there was some sort of mawkish reconciliation. . . . Mclieshes too have grown shadowy—he's *so* nice but she's a club woman at heart and made a great lot of trouble in subtle ways this summer. We saw Marice the day she left and the huge Garoupe standing desolate, and her face, and the pathetic bales of *chiclets* for the Garoupe beach in her bedroom are the strongest impression I have left of a futile and petty summer. It might all have happened at Roslynn Long Island.

Swimmings almost over now. We have our tickets for America Dec. 10th on the Conte Biancamo—we'll spend the winter in New York. Bishop was here with his unspeakably awful wife. He seems aenemic and washed out, a memory of the past so far as I'm concerned.

Im glad as hell about the story and I hope its the first of many. I feel too much at loose ends to write any more tonight. Remember—if I can give you any financial help let me know.

Always Your Friend
Scott—

I had a lot more to say but its 3.30 A.M. and Ive been working since 11 this morning and its very hazy. Have you read

The Spanish Farm	⎫	by Mottram
+	⎬	
Sixty four—ninety four	⎭	?

Wonderful war books. Much better than Ford Maddox Ford. In fact the best thing I've read this summer. Met your cousin from Princeton!

Late in 1926, when the Fitzgeralds were preparing to leave Juan-les-Pins for America, Hemingway wrote from Paris saying that his trip to Marseilles didn't work out. Scott is the only man in or out of Europe he wants to see. In this euphoric letter written after publication of *The Sun Also Rises* on 22 October Ernest claims that in gratitude to Scott he is going to insert a subtitle in the eighth printing of the novel:

THE SUN ALSO RISES (LIKE YOUR COCK IF YOU HAVE ONE)
A Greater Gatsby
(Written with the friendship of F. Scott FitzGerald
(Prophet of THE JAZZ AGE)

Ernest boasts about his decency where money is concerned and admits that he has been sucked in to do good writing by ambition. He is very poor and eating only one meal a day, but has gotten over a suicidal phase in connection with his separation from Hadley. He describes himself as a son-of-a-bitch.

Before leaving the Riviera Fitzgerald sent Hemingway a note offering help.

Villa St. Louis
Juan-les-Pins

Dear Ernest:
We leave this house Tuesday for Genoa + New York. I hope everything's going better for you. If there is anything you need done here or in America—anything about your work, or money, or human help under any head, remember you can always call on
Your Devoted Friend
Scott

Fitzgerald followed this note with a letter written aboard the *Conte Biancammano* but mailed from Washington on 23 December 1926.

[54]

Dear Ernest=

Your letter depressed me—illogicly because I knew more or less what was coming. I wish I could have seen you + heard you, if you wished, give some sort of version of what happened to you. Anyhow I'm sorry for you and for Hadley + for Bumby and I hope some way you'll all be content and things will not seem so hard and bad.

I can't tell you how much your friendship has meant to me during this year and a half—it is the brightest thing in our trip to Europe for me. I will try to look out for your interests with Scribner in America, but I gather that the need of that is past now and that soon you'll be financially more than on your feet.

I'm sorry you didn't come to Marseille. I go back with my novel still unfinished and with less health + not much more money than when I came, but somehow content, for the moment, with motion and New York ahead and Zelda's entire recovery[5]—and happy about the amount of my book that I've already written.

I'm delighted with what press I've already seen of *The Sun ect.* Did not realize you had stolen at all from me but am prepared to believe that its true + shall tell everyone. By the way I liked it in print even better than in manuscript.

1st Printing was probably 5000. 2nd Printing may mean that they've sold 4,500 so have ordered up 3000 more. It may mean any sale from 2500 to 5000, tho.

College Humor pays fine. No movie in *Sun Also* unless book is big success of scandal. That's just a guess.

We all enjoyed "la vie est beau avec Papa". We agree with Bumby.

Always Yours Affectionately,

Scott

Write me care of Scribners.

Fitzgerald's letter includes nothing about Hemingway's forthcoming marriage to Pauline Pfeiffer. It is unlikely that Fitzgerald did not know about Hemingway's marriage plans, since his involvement with Pauline was hardly a secret by this time. Fitzgerald did not approve of Pauline—a feeling she reciprocated.

5 From colitis, appendicitis, and an ovarian problem.

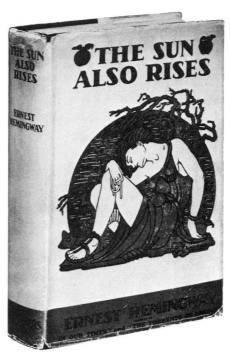

The Sun Also Rises had been widely and receptively reviewed. The first printing of 5090 copies sold fast, and it was reprinted in November, December, January 1927, February (twice), March. By November 1929 it was in its tenth printing. Hemingway did not receive any of the royalties because he assigned the novel to Hadley as a divorce settlement—although he subsequently recovered the rights to the novel.

Early in 1927 Fitzgerald was visiting his parents in Washington and trying to heal some sort of grudge Hemingway was nurturing against H. L. Mencken, editor of *The American Mercury* and the most influential critic of the time.

Address Scribners

Dear Ernest:

    A line in terrible haste. Lunched with Mencken in Baltimore yesterday. He is just starting reading *The Sun* ect—has no recollection of having seen *Big Two Hearted River* + admits confusion about two *In Our* Times. Got him to say he'd pay you $250. for anything of yours he could use. So there's another market.

Told him about how you were going to beat him up. He's a "peach of a fellow" (no irony, just a slip of the pen. He's thoroughly interested + utterly incapable of malice. Whole thing was simply rather sloppy, as he's one of the busiest men in America

The Killers was fine.

                                    Yr. Devoted Friend
                                                Scott

The feud simmering between Hemingway and Mencken was one-sided. Mencken had not yet reviewed any of Hemingway's books, which may have been what was bothering Hemingway. ("How to Waste Material," Fitzgerald's essay-review of *In Our Time*, had been declined by *The American Mercury*.) However, the *Mercury* ridiculed the Paris *in our time* with an unsigned brief notice in August 1925. Since this notice appeared more than a year after the publication of *in our time*, there is a chance that Fitzgerald may have called the volume to Mencken's attention as part of his campaign to promote Hemingway's career. The *Mercury* comment, which appeared under the heading "Quackery," read in full:

> The sort of brave, bold stuff that all atheistic young newspaper reporters write. Jesus Christ in lower case. A hanging, a carnal love, and two disembowelings. Here it is set forth solemnly on Rives hand-made paper, in an edition of 170 copies, and with the imprimatur of Ezra Pound.

The style is straight Mencken, and Hemingway was almost certainly correct in attributing the sneer to the Baltimore Anti-Christ.

By 1927 Mencken had ignored two salvos from Hemingway which were invitations to counterattack. *The Torrents of Spring* had been satirically dedicated "TO H. L. MENCKEN AND S. STANWOOD MENCKEN IN ADMIRATION." Since S. Stanwood Menken (which was the correct spelling) was a reformer who represented some of the things H. L. Mencken ridiculed, coupling their names was intended to be incongruous—not "in admiration." *The Sun Also Rises* included a ludicrous reference to Mencken in Bill Gorton's nonsense humor: "Remember the woods were God's first temples. Let us kneel and say: 'Don't eat that, Lady—that's Mencken.' " It is a fair inference that Hemingway—who had not had any contact with Mencken—was using an old ploy of ambitious young writers by attacking a prominent literary figure. If so, it didn't work because Mencken did not respond.

Fitzgerald wanted these two writers he greatly admired to admire each other, and he particularly wanted Mencken to give favorable notice to Hemingway. Fitzgerald subsequently presented Mencken with an inscribed copy of *Men Without Women,* Hemingway's second story collection, when it was published in 1927:

> Dear Menk:
>   Please read this—at least read *The Killers Pursuit Race + Now I lay me*
>   He's really a great writer, since Anderson's collapse the best we have I think.   Ever yours
> Scott Fitz—

Fitzgerald's efforts may have prompted Mencken to review *Men Without Women* in the May 1928 *American Mercury.* Pairing Hemingway with Thornton Wilder, he commented, "It is technical virtuosity that has won them attention; it is hard work and fundamental thinking that must get them on, if they are to make good their high promise."

On 31 March 1927 Hemingway wrote from Paris thanking Fitzgerald for his efforts to promote his work and reporting Harold Loeb's reaction to seeing himself thinly disguised as Robert Cohn in *The Sun Also Rises.* After Loeb announced he was going to shoot him, Ernest passed the word that he would be waiting at Lipp's brasserie on the Boulevard St. Germain for two afternoons; but Loeb did not show up. Harold Loeb has denied that he ever threatened to shoot Hemingway. Ernest ridicules Louis Bromfield's novels and describes a bad dinner at Bromfield's home during which he was tempted to piss in the finger bowls. He got Scott's cable about writing for *Vanity Fair,* but has decided not to write anything to order because that wastes material. However, Scott has suggested a subject that would not be jacking off to write, and Ernest will try to do something with it. Nothing by Hemingway appeared

"Ellerslie"—with Fitzgerald's caption for Hemingway. Ernest Hemingway Collection, John F. Kennedy Library.

in *Vanity Fair*. The letter includes Hemingway's warm expressions of gratitude to Fitzgerald, calling him his best friend and saying that his feelings about Scott are so strong that he can't write about them. "You do more and work harder and oh shit I'd get maudlin about how damned swell you are."

After a wasted Hollywood trip the Fitzgeralds settled at "Ellerslie," a mansion near Wilmington, Delaware, which they rented from March 1927 to March 1929. Fitzgerald had gone to Hollywood to make fast money by writing an original "flapper" screenplay for Constance Talmadge; but it was rejected and he received only the down-payment. On 18 April 1927 Fitzgerald wrote to Hemingway, who was in Paris awaiting his May marriage to Pauline Pfeiffer:

> God! Those terrible Bromfields! I recognized the parsimonious dinner
> Dear Ernest:
> Your stories[6] were great (in April Scribner). But like me you must beware Conrad rythyms in direct quotation from characters especially if you're pointing a single phrase + making a man live by it.

[6] "In Another Country" and "Canary for One."

"In the fall the war was always there but we did not go to it any more" is one of the most beautiful prose sentences I've ever read.

So much has happened to me lately that I despair of ever assimilating it—or for forgetting it which is the same thing.

I hate to think of your being hard up. Please use this if it would help. The Atlantic will pay about $200, I suppose. I'll get in touch with Perkins about it when he returns from vacation (1 wk.). Won't they advance you all you need on the bk of stories? Your title [*Men Without Women*] is fine by the way. What chance of yr. crossing this summer?

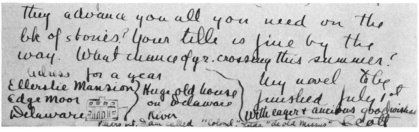

Ernest Hemingway Collection, John F. Kennedy Library

After his second marriage Hemingway would not need loans. Pauline Pfeiffer was thirty-one, three years older than he. She was a devout Catholic, and Hemingway became a practicing Catholic at the time of their marriage—claiming that he had been baptized by a priest after his wounding in 1918. The daughter of a wealthy Arkansas landowner, she had been working for the Paris edition of *Vogue*. Some of her friends thought that Pauline's real activity in Paris was husband-hunting. In addition to her own financial prospects, she enjoyed the generosity of her rich uncle, Gustavus Adolphus Pfeiffer, who was the controlling stockholder in Richard Hudnut cosmetics. After their marriage Hemingway's lifestyle expanded considerably. Although his books sold well, his royalties did not support the way the Hemingways lived—their house in Key West, their summers in Wyoming, their trips to Europe.

Fitzgerald's April letter did not catch up with Hemingway until the summer. In late July or August Hemingway wrote from

Ernest and Pauline Hemingway.

Spain thanking Scott for the $100 loan, to be repaid after *Men Without Women* was published in October. As a binder on a contract for ten stories the Hearst magazines sent Ernest a check for $1000, which he returned. Ernest reports with annoyance that Fanny Butcher of the *Chicago Tribune* has called Louis Bromfield the American Fielding. The latest news about the originals for the *Sun Also Rises* characters is that Duff Twysden got her divorce, but Pat Guthrie won't marry her because she has lost her looks. Duff kidnapped her son from England and is keeping him in the south of France. She is not angry about *Sun,* but says she never slept with the bullfighter.

Through the fall of 1927 Maxwell Perkins sent Hemingway concerned letters about Fitzgerald's nervous state and his inability to get on with his novel. He visited "Ellerslie" and is worried that Scott may have a breakdown. Perkins has persuaded Scott to switch to Sano cigarettes—making the colossal mis-diagnosis that "tobacco was hurting him more than drink." Hemingway responded expressing concern, saying that he wished he could come over and put Scott back in shape.

In October 1927 Scott wrote from "Ellerslie" to Ernest in Paris congratulating him on *Men Without Women:*

Dear Ernest:

Thousands will send you this clipping.[7] I should think it would make you quite conscious of your public existence. Its well meant—he praised your book a few days before.

The book is fine. I like it quite as well as *The Sun,* which doesn't begin to express my entheusiasm. In spite of all its geographical + emotional rambling, its a unit, as much as Conrad's books of Contes were. Zelda read it with facination, liking it better than anything you've written. Her favorite was *Hills like White Elephants,* mine, barring *The Killers* was *Now I Lay Me.* The one about the Indians ["Ten Indians"] was the only one that left me cold and I'm glad you left out *Up in Michigan.*[8] They probably belong to an earlier + almost exhaused vein.

"In the fall the war was always there but we did not go to it anymore." God, what a beautiful line. And the waking dreams in *Now I Lay me* and the whole mood of *Hills Like."*

Did you see the pre-review by that cocksucker Rascoe[9] who obviously had read only three stories but wanted to be up to the minute?

Max says its almost exhausted 7500—however that was five days ago. I like your title—*All the Sad Young Men Without Women*—and I feel my influence is beginning to tell. Manuel Garcia is obviously Gatsby. What you havn't learned from me you'll get from Good

<hr />

7 A parody of Hemingway in F.P.A.'s "Conning Tower" column.
8 On 10 May, Perkins had asked Fitzgerald's advice about publishing "Up in Michigan," the story that Liveright had earlier declined to publish in *In Our Time.* Fitzgerald replied on the 12th: "One line *at least* is pornographic, though *please* don't bring my name into the discussion. The thing is—what is a seduction story with the seduction left out. Yet if that is softened it is quite printable."
9 Burton Rascoe, *Bookman* (September 1927).

Woman Bromfield and soon you'll be Marching in the Van of the Younger Generation.

No work this summer but lots this fall. Hope to finish the novel by 1st December. Have got nervous as hell lately—purely physical but scared me somewhat—to the point of putting me on the wagon and smoking denicotinized cigarettes. Zelda is ballet dancing three times a week with the Phila symphony—painting also. I think you were wise not jumping at Hearsts offer. I had a contract with them that, as it turned out, did me unspeakable damage in one way or another. Long[10] is a sentimental scavenger with no ghost of taste or individuality, not nearly so much as Lorimer[11] for example. However, why not send your stories to Paul Reynolds? He'll be glad to handle them + will get you good prices. The *Post* now pays me $3500.—this detail so you'll be sure who's writing this letter.

I can't tell you how I miss you. May cross for 6 wks in March or April. *The Grandmothers*[12] was respectable but undistinguished, and are you coming home. Best to Pauline. With good wishes + Affection

Scott

Hemingway was skiing at Gstaad—a considerable cut above Schruns socially—in December 1927 / January 1928 and sent Fitzgerald a torn letter that was too dull to mail, but which he doesn't have the energy to rewrite. He reports that he wrote twenty chapters (60,000 words) of his next novel before breaking off because of physical problems. (Hemingway's 60,000 words were for a "modern Tom Jones," which he abandoned to start *A Farewell to Arms* in March 1928.) Bumby poked him in the eye, temporarily blinding him; his other ailments include grippe, piles, and a toothache. Although Fitzgerald was pleased by Hemingway's success, the news that Ernest was working so prolifically must have caused a painful assessment of his failure to complete his own novel.

10 Hearst magazine editor Ray Long.
11 George Horace Lorimer, editor of *The Saturday Evening Post*.
12 Glenway Wescott's novel.

Hemingway's letter may have crossed Fitzgerald's December 1927 sanguine prediction about his novel:

> Ellerslie
> Edgemoor
> Delaware

Dear Ernest:

Perkins send me the check for 800 bits (as we westerners say), indicating I hope, that you are now comfortably off in your own ascetic way. I am almost through my novel, got short and had to do three Post stories but as I am now their pet exhibit and go down on them to the tune of 32,000 bits per felony it didn't take long to come to the surface.

(This tough talk is not really characteristic of me— its the influence of *All the Sad Young Men Without Women in Love*.) Louis Golding stepped off the boat + said you and I were the hope of American Letters (if you can find them) but aside from that things look black, "old pard"—Brommy [Bromfield] is sweeping the west, Edna Ferber is sweeping the east and Paul Rosenfeld is sweeping what's left into a large ornate wastebasket, a gift which any Real Man would like, to be published in November under the title: *The Real Liesure Class,* containing the work of one-story Balzacs and poets so thin-skinned as to be moved by everything to exactly the same degree of mild remarking.

Lately I've enjoyed *Some People,*[13] *Bismark* (Ludwig's), *Him*[14] (in parts) and the *Memoirs* of Ludendorff. I have a new German war book, *Die Krieg against Krieg,* which shows men who mislaid their faces in Picardy and the Caucasus—you can imagine how I thumb it over, my mouth fairly slithering with facination.

If you write anything in the line of an "athletic" story please try the *Post* or let me try them for you, or Reynolds. You were wise not to tie up with Hearst's. They are absolute bitches who feed on contracts like vultures, if I may coin a neat simile.

[13] By Harold Nicolson.
[14] By E. E. Cummings.

I've tasted no alcohol for a month but Xmas is coming.

Please write me at length about your adventures—I hear you were seen running through Portugal in used B.V.D.s, chewing ground glass and collecting material for a story about Boule players; that you were publicity man for Lindberg; that you have finished a novel a hundred thousand words long consisting entirely of the word "balls" used in new groupings; that you have been naturalized a Spaniard, dress always in a wine-skin with "zipper" vent and are engaged in bootlegging Spanish Fly between St. Sebastian and Biaritz where your agents sprinkle it on the floor of the Casino. I hope I have been misformed but, alas!, it all has too true a ring. For your own good I should be back there, with both of us trying to be good fellows at a terrible rate. Just before you pass out next time think of me.

This is a wowsy country but France is swehw and I hope to spend March and April, or April and May, there and elsewhere on the continent.

How are you, physically and mentally? Do you sleep? *Now I Lay Me* was a fine story—you ought to write a companion piece, *Now I Lay Her*. Excuse my bawdiness but I'm oversexed and am having saltpetre put in my *Pâté de Foie Gras au Truffles Provênçal*.

Please write news. My best to Pauline—Zelda's also to you both. God will forgive everybody—even Robert McAlmon and Burton Rascoe.

Always afftly
Scott

In an undated 1927 letter Hemingway wrote to Fitzgerald that Bromfield has met his mother on a lecture tour, so that now Mrs. Hemingway is no doubt regretting the fact that her son doesn't write like Bromfield. Ernest claims that Bumby—who was four—has received an offer from Hearst to write a novel about Lesbians who were wounded in the war. While Hemingway was beginning *A Farewell to Arms*, Fitzgerald was still stuck on his novel, which he interrupted to write short stories. In 1927–28 he published twelve stories, ten of which were in *The Saturday Evening Post*. His earnings in 1927 were $29,000 and in 1928 $25,000—including more than $7,000 in advances for the novel. Fitzgerald's drinking behavior became increasingly erratic, and his domestic situation became increasingly strained. Zelda Fitzgerald's ambition for her own career prompted her to begin intense ballet training at the advanced age of twenty-seven; and her absorption in her lessons caused an estrangement between the Fitzgeralds. Now it was Scott who wanted to party when Zelda wanted to work.

In March 1928 Hemingway was hit in the head by a falling skylight in the toilet of his Paris apartment. Nine stitches were required, leaving a permanent scar on his forehead. Fitzgerald was in America when the accident occurred and was not involved in any way. Nonetheless, the extent of the legendizing activity that has been generated around these figures is revealed by a false report of the accident in which Fitzgerald is the villain. In 1956–57 Jed Kiley, a former editor of the Paris *Boulevardier,* wrote a series of reminiscences about Hemingway for *Playboy,* which became a book entitled *Hemingway: An Old Friend Remembers* (1965). Kiley attributed to Fitzgerald the claim that he had deliberately pulled down the skylight in an attempt to kill Hemingway. Apart from the circumstance that such an action was extremely unlikely for Fitzgerald to commit against a friend he virtually worshipped, geography made it impossible. It is, however, remotely possible that Fitzgerald may have made this claim to Kiley, for he made wild statements when he was drunk. Kiley's unverified account gained considerable currency before it was rebutted by Archibald MacLeish's letter to the London *Times Literary Supplement.* MacLeish, who took Hemingway to the hospital after the accident, stated that Fitzgerald was in no way involved. Hemingway's own report to Perkins of 17 March 1928 makes it clear that he was alone in the toilet when he tried to hook up a cord that a guest had pulled by mistake, bringing the skylight down on his head.

During 1928 Hemingway and Perkins exchanged concerned letters about Fitzgerald, with speculations about his progress on the novel. On 21 April Hemingway wrote Perkins from Key West developing his theory that Scott had been blocked by the reviews of *The Great Gatsby*—especially by Gilbert Seldes' review—which made him afraid not to write a great novel. The thing for Scott to do is write; he could have finished three novels in the time since *Gatsby*. Perkins replied that he doesn't think Fitzgerald is attempting the impossible with his novel. The problem is Zelda's extravagance. They ought to get a housekeeper to manage them.

The Fitzgeralds spent the spring and summer of 1928 in Paris, a wasted time of drinking for Fitzgerald. Fitzgerald wrote Hemingway, probably in July, joking about Hemingway's conversion to Catholicism. Fitzgerald was a lapsed Catholic and never showed any concern about it.

> Teenie-weenie Corner
> Sunshineville.

Precious Papa, Bull-fighter, Gourmand ect.

It has come to my ears

(a) That you have been seen bycycling through Kansas, chewing + spitting a mixture of goat's meat + chicory which the natives collect + sell for artery-softener and market-glut

(b) That Bumby has won the Benjamin Altman scholarship at Cundle School + taken first prizes in *Comparitive Epistemology, Diseases of Cormorants + Small Vultures, Amateur Gyncology + Intestinal Hysterics*

(c) That you are going to fight Jim Tully in Washdog Wisconsin on Decoration Day in a chastity belt with your hair cut á la garconne.

Is it all true?

We are friends with the Murphys again. Talked about you a great deal + while we *tried* to say only kind things we managed to get in a few good cracks that would amuse you—about anybody else—which is what you get for being so far away. Incidently called twice on Hadley— she was both times out but saw Bumby once + think he's the best kid I ever saw by 1000 miles.

Well, old Mackerel Snatcher, wolf a Wafer + + a Beaker of blood for me,—and when you come Shadowboxing into my life again with your new similes for

"swewa" and "wousy" (which, as you doubtless notice, you've given to the world) no one will be glader than your
                                            Devoted Friend
                                            Scott Fitzg—

While in America don't cast any doubt on my statement that you held a bridgehead (or was it a hophead) at Caporetto for three days + utterly baffled the 2nd Austrian Army Corps. In 50 yrs all the people that could have denied it will be dead or busy holding their own bridgeheads—like Lawrence Stallings, who is slowly taking to himself the communal exploits of the 5th + 6th Marines. "Hebuterne—of course I know it—I took that village."
    Do send Lorimer a story. I Read Mencken's public apology. Not bad for an old man who has had his troubles. God help us all! Have seen a good deal of Joyce. Please come back—will be here till Aug 20TH 58 Rue de Vaugirard. Then back to America for a few months.
                                            Best to Pauline!

    In the fall of 1928 Hemingway wrote Fitzgerald from Piggott, Arkansas, saying that he finished *A Farewell to Arms* a month ago and expressing incredulity about Perkins' report that Scott is writing eight hours a day. Ernest writes only two hours a day. As a result of the birth of Patrick—the first of his two sons by Pauline—Ernest plans to offer counseling on how to produce perfect babies. On the 11th of October Hemingway wrote Perkins an angry letter about Zelda's influence on Scott. He often thinks Scott might have been the greatest of American writers if he had not married her. No writer has ever had more talent—or squandered his talent more.
    In November 1928 Fitzgerald and Hemingway had their first reunion since the summer of 1926. The Hemingways and artist Mike Strater met the Fitzgeralds at Princeton on the 19th for the Yale-Princeton game. Ernest's account of this meeting is preserved in a four-page unfinished chapter for *A Moveable Feast*. Fitzgerald had remained sober at the game. After the game they all took the train to Philadelphia, where they were met by the Fitzgeralds' chauffeur with their Buick and driven to "Ellerslie," outside of

Wilmington. On the train Fitzgerald gets drunk and annoys people, particularly a medical student he insists is a clap doctor. During the drive to "Ellerslie" the chauffeur—a former Paris taxi driver Fitzgerald had brought to America—complains to Ernest that Fitzgerald won't let him put any oil in the car. Fitzgerald overhears the chauffeur and insists that American cars do not require additional oil—unlike the Renault that he and Hemingway had driven from Lyons to Paris in 1925. The chapter breaks off with the Fitzgeralds' arguing about the turn-off to their house. The Hemingways spent the night at "Ellerslie" and left for Chicago on "The Spirit of St. Louis" the next day.

There is another account of this reunion in A. E. Hotchner's *Papa Hemingway* (1966), which Hotchner presents as told to him by Hemingway. In this version Hemingway went alone to dine with the Fitzgeralds in their mansion outside *Baltimore*. He was met at the station by the chauffeur, Pierre (his name was Philippe), with "a custom-built Hotchkiss" which Fitzgerald would not lubricate. At dinner Fitzgerald was drunk and unpleasant before passing out. There was no one to drive Hemingway to the station, so he had to spend the night instead of returning to New York to work on proofs with Perkins. The next day Fitzgerald tried to prevent Hemingway from catching the "one train a day" from Baltimore to New York. In the car on the way to the station Fitzgerald—petulant because Hemingway was leaving—kicked out the windshield and cut his foot. "Scott turned savagely abusive and hysterical and I had to slap his face hard to quiet him down." The checkable details in Hotchner's account do not check out. In 1928 the Fitzgeralds were living at "Ellerslie," near Wilmington; Hemingway never visited them at "La Paix" near Baltimore, where they lived in 1932–33. Fitzgerald never owned a Hotchkiss—custom-built or otherwise—which was a very expensive French car; at "Ellerslie" they had a Buick, as Hemingway correctly notes in his own account.

After the "Ellerslie" visit, Hemingway wrote a bread-and-butter letter on the train thanking Fitzgerald for a good time and apologizing for having been a nuisance about getting to the train on time. There was some unexplained trouble with a policeman at the station. While Scott was in the hands of the law, Ernest called from the platform phone and explained to the cop that Scott is a great writer, and the cop replied that Scott says the same thing about Ernest.[15]

On 6 December 1928 Hemingway was southbound from New York to Key West with Bumby on the "Havana Special." At Trenton, New Jersey, he received a wire informing him that his father had died in Oak Park. Hemingway wired Perkins to send $100 to the North Philadelphia station; but there was no reply, so he wired both Fitzgerald and Strater. Fitzgerald delivered the money to North Philadelphia. Suffering from diabetes and angina and under financial pressure because of bad investments in Florida real estate, Dr. Hemingway had shot himself. Hemingway blamed his mother, feeling her domination had unmanned his father.

Hemingway wrote to Fitzgerald from the train on the way back to Key West after the funeral saying that he is too sick about his father's suicide to write a proper letter but wants to thank him for his help. Fitzgerald replied on the 28th of December:

> Dear Ernest:
>
> I'm terribly sorry about your trouble. I guess losing parents is just one of the things that happens to one in the thirties—every time I see my father now I think its the last time.
>
> Thank Pauline for the really beautiful Xmas card. It was great to have you both here, even when I was intermittently unconscious.
>
> I send you what may be news, and what a nice precedent for beating up Mencken.[16] Saw the Murphys for an hour in New York. We're sailing March 1st + I hope to have the novel here. (Confidential about sailing though until I'm sure—won't go unless novel's finished.) Ring [Lardner] thought you were fine—he was uncharacteristicly entheusiastic.
>
> I'm bored + somewhat depressed tonight so I won't

---

15 A third report of the Hemingways' visit to "Ellerslie" is in Sara Mayfield's *Exiles from Paradise*. She reports that Zelda Fitzgerald was disturbed by Hemingway's "jokes with Scott about pederasty, anal eroticism, and other forms of perversion"; and that Fitzgerald and Hemingway got drunk and were jailed after a brawl. Miss Mayfield was not present, and there is no supporting evidence for her account.
16 A newspaper clipping, "Toreador Is Barred for Beating Up Critic."

continue. Oh, yes—I met old H. Stearns just before leaving Paris and feeling drunk and Christ-like suggested a title to him: "Why I go on being poor in Paris", told him to write it as an informal letter to me and I'd sell it.[17] In a burst of energy he did + I sent it to Max who wrote a check for $100.00 for it. Now Harold writes me that $100 isn't very much (as a matter of fact, it isn't much of a letter either) and exhibits such general dissatisfaction that I think he thinks I held out on him. You've got to be careful who you do favors for—within a year you'll probably hear a story that what started him on his downward path was my conscienceless theft of his royaties.

Spengler's second volume[18] is marvellous. Nothing else is any good—when will you save me from the risk of memorizing your works from over-reading them by finishing another? Remember, Proust is dead—to the great envy of

Your Crony and Gossip
Scott

Edgemoor
Delaware

17 "Apologia of an Expatriate," *Scribner's Magazine,* 85 (March 1929), pp. 338–341.
18 *The Decline of the West.*

III

Fitzgerald's novel was not finished in March 1929, but the Fitzgeralds gave up "Ellerslie" and went to France. The Hemingways were in Paris, and when Hemingway heard that the Fitzgeralds were definitely coming, he instructed Perkins not to give Fitzgerald his address. Scott got him thrown out of one Paris apartment by fighting with the landlord, pissing on the porch, and trying to break down the door at 3 or 4 A.M. Ernest wants to see Scott in public places but doesn't want him in his apartment. The news that Scott is coming to Paris gives Ernest the horrors.

Expecting to see a great deal of Hemingway in Paris, Fitzgerald was hurt to find that Ernest's address was kept from him; he was forced to communicate with Hemingway by sending messages c/o Pauline's sister, Virginia. A list of "Snubs" Fitzgerald made in his *Notebooks* includes "Ernest apartment." Fitzgerald's eagerness to be with Hemingway is shown by this May 1929 note inviting the Hemingways to dinner:

Dear Herr Hemophile: or "Bleeding Boy" as I sometimes call you.
    Will you take salt with us Sun. or Mon. night? would make great personal whoopee on reciept of favorable response. Send me a pneu or answer in person, save between

3 + 7, Highest references, willing to [tra]vel—gens du
monde, cultivee, sympathetique cherche hote pour di-
manche ou lundi—answer because I shall prob. ask
Bishop, if you can come—he is new man without frau.

The encounters between Fitzgerald and Hemingway during
spring-summer 1929 generated new strains from which their friendship never recovered. Fitzgerald was drinking heavily and was de-
fensive about his unfinished novel—despite the optimistic reports
he had sent Hemingway. The animosity between Zelda and Ernest
was compounded by Pauline's disapproval of the Fitzgeralds. Fitzgerald had other reasons to be unhappy besides his guilt about his
work. His marriage was becoming increasingly troubled. Zelda's
intense ballet efforts in Paris left her strained and fatigued, and her
behavior became markedly erratic. The Fitzgeralds were having
sexual problems. Fitzgerald complained of her indifference, and
Zelda countercharged that he was an unsatisfactory lover. It was
probably at this time that Fitzgerald sought Hemingway's sexual
counsel. As recounted in "A Matter of Measurements" in *A Moveable Feast,* Fitzgerald set up a lunch at Michaud's and told Hemingway that Zelda complained that his penis was too small to satisfy
her. Ernest checked Scott's anatomy in the toilet and assured him
that the organ was normal. Scott remained unconvinced, so Ernest
took him to the Louvre and showed him the nude male statues. Ernest advised Scott to recover his confidence by sleeping with another

woman: " 'Forget what Zelda said' I told him. 'Zelda is crazy. There's nothing wrong with you. Just have a little confidence and do what the girl wants. Zelda just wants to destroy you.' " Even though he obviously trusted Hemingway's discretion, Fitzgerald should have realized that an admission of sexual insecurity would inevitably damage him with Hemingway. It is a gauge of Fitzgerald's anxiety and his admiration for Hemingway's masculine prowess that he sought his advice.[19]

Fitzgerald leaves the Louvre to meet some people at the Ritz Bar. Then Hemingway reports a conversation with Georges, the head barman at the Ritz, some twenty-five years later. Georges was puzzled by the tourists who asked him about "this Monsieur Fitzgerald," whom he could not remember. In some way Hemingway regarded Fitzgerald's sexual insecurity to be as significant as his failure to impress himself on the Ritz barman. (The best writing about the Ritz Bar is in *Tender Is the Night* and "Babylon Revisited.")

Fitzgerald probably kept from Hemingway Zelda's accusations that they were involved in a homosexual affair. When Fitzgerald had muttered "No more baby" in his drunken sleep after a meeting with Hemingway, Zelda interpreted it as proof of the liaison. Instead of dismissing Zelda's charges, Fitzgerald apparently began to worry about his possible latent homosexuality—or at least was concerned about acquiring that reputation. The young Canadian novelist Morley Callaghan was in Paris in 1929, where he saw a good deal of both Fitzgerald and Hemingway. Callaghan was also a Scribners author, having been recommended to Perkins by both Fitzgerald and Hemingway. His memoir, *That Summer in Paris* (1963), includes this comment by Fitzgerald: "Remember the night I was in bad shape? I took your arm. Well, I dropped it. It was like holding a dead fish. You thought I was a fairy, didn't you?"

In 1930 after Zelda had been hospitalized in Switzerland, Fitzgerald wrote a long analysis of their marriage in the form of a letter, but it is unlikely that he ever sent it to her.

---

19 After *Feast* was published, Arnold Gingrich and Sheilah Graham testified that Fitzgerald's penis was normal. Gingrich, the editor of *Esquire,* had noticed it when Fitzgerald's bathrobe fell open. Miss Graham was Fitzgerald's lover during the last three years of his life.

I know this then—that those days when we came up from the south, from Capri, were among my happiest—but you were sick and the happiness was not in the home.

I had been unhappy for a long time then—When my play failed a year and a half before, when I worked so hard for a year, twelve stories and novel and four articles in that time with no one believing in me and no one to see except you + before the end your heart betraying me and then I was really alone with no one I liked In Rome we were dismal and was still working proof and three more stories and in Capri you were sick and there seemed to be nothing left of happiness in the world anywhere I looked.

Then we came to Paris and suddenly I realized that it hadn't all been in vain. I was a success—the biggest man in my profession everybody admired me and I was proud I'd done such a good thing. I met Gerald and Sara who took us for friends now and Ernest who was an equeal and my kind of an idealist. I got drunk with him on the Left Bank in careless cafes and drank with Sara and Gerald in their garden in St Cloud but you were endlessly sick and at home everything was unhappy. We went to Antibes and I was happy but you were sick still and all that fall and that winter and spring at the cure and I was alone all the time and I had to get drunk before I could leave you so sick and not care and I was only happy a little before I got too drunk. Afterwards there were all the usuall penalties for being drunk.

Finally you got well in Juan-les-Pins and a lot of money came in and I made of those mistakes literary men make—I thought I was "a man of the world—that everybody liked me and admired me for myself but I only liked a few people like Ernest and Charlie McArthur and Gerald and Sara who were my peers. Time goes bye fast in those moods and nothing is ever done. I thought then that things came easily—I forgot how I'd dragged the Great Gatsby out of the pit of my stomach in a time of misery. I woke up in Hollywood no longer my egotistic, certain self but a mixture of Ernest in fine clothes and Gerald with a career—and Charlie McArthur with a past. Anybody that could make me believe that, like Lois Moran did, was precious to me.

Ellerslie, the polo people Mrs. Chandler the party for Cecelia were all attempts to make up from without for being undernourished now from within. Anything to be liked, to be reassured not that I was a man of a little genius but that I was a great man of the world. At the same time I knew it was nonsense—the part of me that knew it was nonsense brought us to the Rue Vaugirard.

But now you had gone into yourself just as I had four years before in St. Raphael—And there were all the consequences of bad appartments through your lack of patience ("Well, if you were [indecipherable] why don't you make some money") bad servants through your indifference ("Well, if you don't like her why don't you send Scotty away to school") Your dislike for Vidor, your indifference to Joyce I understood—share your incessant entheusisam and absorbtion in the ballet I could not. Somewhere in there I had a sense of being exploited, not by you but by something I resented terribly no happiness. Certainly less than there had ever been at home—you were a phantom washing clothes, talking French bromides with Lucien or Del Plangue I remember desolate trips to Versaille to Rhiems, to La Baule undertaken in sheer weariness of home. I remember wondering why I kept working to pay the bills of this desolate menage. I had evolved. In despair I went from the extreme of isolation, which is to say isolation with Mlle Delplangue, or the Ritz Bar where I got back my self esteem for half an hour, often with someone I had hardly ever seen before. In the evenings sometimes you and I rode to the Bois in a cab—after awhile I preferred to go to Cafe de Lilas and sit there alone remembering what a happy time I had had there with Ernest, Hadley, Dorothy Parker + Benchley two years before. During all this time, remember I didn't blame anyone but myself. I complained when the house got unbearable but after all I was not John Peale Bishop—I was paying for it with work, that I passionately hated and found more and more difficult to do. The novel was like a dream, daily farther and farther away.

Ellerslie was better and worse. Unhappiness is less

acute when one lives with a certain sober dignity but the financial strain was too much. Between Sept when we left Paris and March when we reached Nice we were living at the rate of forty thousand a year.

But somehow I felt happier. Another spring—I would see Ernest whom I had launched, Gerald + Sarah Murphy who through my agency had been able to try the movies. At least life would less drab; there would be parties with people who offered something, conversations with people with something to say. Later swimming and getting tanned and young and being near the sea.

It worked out beautifully didn't it. Gerald and Sara didn't see us. Ernest and I met but it was a more irritable Ernest, apprehensively telling me his whereabouts lest I come in on them tight and endanger his lease. the discovery that half a dozen people were familiars there didn't help my self esteem. By the time we reached the beautiful Rivierra I had developed such an inferiority complex that I couldn't fase anyone unless I was tight. I worked there too, though, and the unusual combination exploded my lungs

You were gone now—I scarcely remember you that summer. You were simply one of all the people who disliked me or were indifferent to me. I didn't like to think of you—You didn't need me and it was easier to talk to or rather at Madame Bellois and keep full of wine. I was grateful when you came with me to the Doctors one afternoon but after we'd been a week in Paris and I didn't try any more about living or dieing things were always the same. The appartments that were rotten, the maids that stank—the ballet before my eyes, spoiling a story to take the Troubetskoys to dinner, poisening a trip to Africa You were going crazy and calling it genius—I was going to ruin and calling it anything that came to hand. And I think everyone far enough away to see us outside of our glib presentation of ourselves guessed at your almost meglomaniacal selfishness and my insane indulgence in drink. Toward the end nothing much mattered. The nearest I ever came to leaving you was when you told me you thot I was a fairy in the Rue Palatine but now whatever you said aroused a sort of detached pity for you. Remember

[78]

this For all your superior observation and your harder intelligence I have a faculty of guessing right without evidence even with a certain wonder as to why and whence that mental short cut came.

I wish the Beautiful and Damned had been a maturely written book because it was all true. We ruined ourselves—I have never honestly thought that we ruined each other.

At about the same time Zelda reviewed the deterioration of her marriage in a 42-page letter written to Fitzgerald from Prangins sanitarium in 1930. Describing the wretched Paris summers of 1928 and 1929, she blamed Fitzgerald's alcoholism and indicated her resentment of Hemingway's influence:

We lived in the rue de Vaugirard [1928]. You were constantly drunk. You didn't work and were dragged home at night by taxi-drivers when you came home at all. You said it was my fault for dancing all day. What was I to do? You got up for lunch. You made no advances toward me and complained that I was un-responsive. You were literally eternally drunk the whole summer. . . . You were angry when I wouldn't go with you to Mont Matre. You brought drunken under-graduates in to meals when you came home for them, and it made you angry that I didn't care any more. . . . We came back to rue Palantine [1929] and you, in a drunken stupor told me a lot of things that I only half understood: but I understood the dinner we had at Ernests'. Only I didn't understand that it mattered. You left me more and more alone, and though you complained that it was the appartment or the servants or me, you know the real reason you couldn't work was because you were always out half the night and you were sick and you drank constantly.

In 1929, as in 1926, Fitzgerald was eager to read Hemingway's novel in typescript—and again Hemingway was reluctant to have him see it. Fitzgerald was allowed to preview *A Farewell to Arms*— probably in June 1929—only after it had been sent to Scribners. (*A Farewell to Arms* began appearing in installments in the May issue of *Scribner's Magazine.*) Fitzgerald again responded with a long document, which was stronger than the one he had prepared for *The Sun Also Rises.*

114-121 is slow + needs cutting[20]—it hasn't the incisiveness of other short portraits in this book or in yr. other books. The characters too numerous + too much nailed down by gags. *Please* cut! There's absolutely no psycholical justification in introducing those singers—its not even bizarre—if he got stewed with them + in consequence thrown from hospital it would be O.K. At least reduce it to a sharp + self sufficient vignette. It's just rather gassy as it is, I think.

For example—your Englishman on the fishing trip in T.S.A.R. contributes to the tautness of waiting for Brett. You seem to have written this to try to "round out the picture of Milan during the war" during a less inspired moment.

(Arn't the Croats Orthodox Greeks?[21] or some Byzantine Christian Sect—Surely they're not predominantly Mohamedens + you can't say their not Christians

P. 124 *et sequitur*[22]
This is definately *dull*—it's all right to say it was meant all the time + that a novel can't have the finesse of a short story but this has got to. This scene as it is seems to me a shame.
Later I was astonished to find it was only about 750 wds. which only goes to show the pace you set yourself up to that point. Its dull because the war goes further +

20 Chapter 19, pp. 126–129 of *A Farewell to Arms:* The meeting with Meyers and his wife through the conversation with the opera singers and Ettore Moretti. This material is crossed out of Hemingway's typescript, perhaps indicating that he considered cutting it. These notes draw heavily upon Charles Mann's "F. Scott Fitzgerald's Critique of *A Farewell to Arms*," *Fitzgerald/Hemingway Annual 1976.*
21 Chapter 26, p. 189: possibly a reference to the priest's statement, "The Austrians are Christians—except for the Bosnians."
22 Chapter 20, pp. 136 ff.: the account of Frederic and Catherine's day at the races.

further out of sight every minute. "That's the way it was" is no answer—this triumphant proof that races were fixed! —I should put it as *400* word beginning to Chap XXI

Still later Read by itself it has points, but coming on it in the novel I still believe its dull + slow

———

Seems to me a last echo of the war very faint when Catherine is dying and he's drinking beer in the Café.

———

Look over Switzerland stuff for cutting

P. 130[23]—
This is a comedy scene that really becomes offensive for you've trained everyone to read every word—now you make them read the word cooked (+ fucked would be as bad) *one dozen times*. It has ceased to become amusing by the 5th, for they're too packed, + yet the scene has possibilities. Reduced to five or six *cooked* it might have rythm like the word "wops" in one of your early sketches. You're a little hypnotized by yourself here.

133-138[24]
This could stand a good cutting. Sometimes these conversations with her take on a naive quality that wouldn't please you in anyone else's work. Have you read Noel Coward?

Some of its wonderful—about brave man 1000 deaths ect. Couldn't you cut a little?

(ie. 2nd page numbered 129)
129 (NW) Now here's a great scene[25]—your comedy used as part of you + not as mere roll-up-my-sleeves = + pull-off a-tour-de-force as on pages 114-121

[23] Chapter 21, pp. 142–143: Henry's report of the British major's analysis of the war. "Wops" refers to the "Chapter VIII" vignette of *In Our Time*.
[24] Chapter 21, pp. 146–151: the scene in which Catherine announces she is pregnant.
[25] Chapter 22, pp. 152–155: Miss Van Campen's discovery of the empty bottles in Frederic Henry's hospital room.

$\overline{(134)}$[26] Remember the brave expectant illegitimate mother is an <u>old situation</u> + has been exploited by all sorts of people you won't lower yourself to read—so be sure every line rings *new* + has some claim to being in-carnated + inspired truth or you'll have the boys apon you with scorn.

By the way—that buying the pistol is a *wonderful* scene.[27]

    Catherine is too glib, talks too much physically. In cutting their conversations cut some of her speeches rather than his. She is too glib—

    I mean—you're seeing him in a sophisticated way as now you see yourself then—but you're *still* seeing her as you did in 1917 thru nineteen yr. old eyes. In conse-quence unless you make her a bit fatuous occasionally the contrast jars—either the writer is a simple fellow or she's Eleanora Duse disguised as a Red Cross nurse. In one mo-ment you expect her to prophecy the 2nd battle of the Marne— as you probably did then. Where's that desper-ate, half-childish don't-make-me think V.A.D. feeling you spoke to me about? It's there—here—but cut *to* it! Don't try to make her make sense—She probably didn't!

122 ect.[28]

In "Cat in the rain" + in the story about "That's all we do isn't it, go + try new drinks ect," You were really listen-ing to women—here you're only listening to yourself, to your own mind beating out facily a sort of sense that isn't really interesting, Ernest, nor really much except a sort of literary exercise—it seems to me that this ought to be *thoroughly* cut, even re-written.

    (Our poor old friendship probably won't survive this but there you are—better me than some nobody in the Literary Review that doesn't care about you + your future.)

---

[26] Chapter 21, p. 147: "I'm going to have a baby, darling." See note 24.
[27] Chapter 23, pp. 158–159.
[28] Chapter 19, pp. 134–135: Frederic and Catherine's conversation about the rain: "I'm afraid of the rain because sometimes I see me dead in it." The stories "Cat in the Rain" and "Hills Like White Elephants" were in *In Our Time.*

The book, by the way is between 80,000 + 100,000 wds—not 160,000 as you thought

P. 241[29] is one of the best pages you've ever written, I think

P 209- + 219[30] I think if you use word cocksuckers here the book will be suppressed + confiscated within two days of publication.

———————

All this retreat is marvellous the confusion ect.
The scene from 218[31] on is the best in recent fiction

I think 293-294[32] need cutting but perhaps not to be cut altogether.

Why not end the book with that wonderful paragraph on P. 241.[33] It is the most eloquent in the book + could end it rather gently + well.

A beautiful book it is!

Hemingway's annotation—"Kiss my ass EH"—indicates that he was less than pleased by Fitzgerald's critique, which came down hard on Catherine Barkley's glibness and criticized her "brave, expectant, illegitimate mother role" as stale. Hemingway subsequently became convinced that Fitzgerald's advice had been worthless and silly. Writing to Arthur Mizener, Fitzgerald's first biographer, in 1951 Hemingway stated, "I have a letter in which he told me how to make A Farewell to Arms a successful book which included some fifty suggestions including eliminating the officer shooting the sergeant, and bringing in, actually and honestly to

29 Chapter 34, pp. 266–267: Frederic Henry's night soliloquy after his reunion with Catherine at Stresa—"If people bring so much courage to this world the world has to kill them to break them, so of course it kills them." Fitzgerald wrote in the margin of the typescript, "This is one of the most beautiful pages in all English literature." The note was erased, but is still readable.
30 Chapter 30, pp. 228, 238. The word was replaced with dashes in print.
31 Chapter 30, pp. 237–241: Frederic Henry's arrest by the carabiniere and his escape.
32 Opening of Chapter 40. This passage was cut by Hemingway. See p. 84.
33 Chapter 34. See note 29.

God, the U.S. Marines (Lt. Henry reads of their success at Belleau Woods while in the Cafe when Catherine is dying) at the end." In 1953 Hemingway sent a report of Fitzgerald's memo to Charles Poore, who was editing *The Hemingway Reader,* stating that Fitzgerald wanted him to incorporate the news of the Marines at

(6)

FINCA VIGIA, SAN FRANCISCO DE PAULA, CUBA

In Château Thierry. This, Scott said, would make the American public understand the book better. He also did not like the scene in the old Hotel Cavour in Milano and wanted changes to be made in many other places "to make it more acceptable." Not one suggestion made the least sense or was useful (he never said this was useful) (this comes under being lonely when you have the point) > had learned not to show them to him a long time before. Will tell you about that some day; too long to write now when am trying to give you the [what] you need. For Whom The Bell Tolls was written here and in Sun Valley Idaho then here. Scribner's files will show the dates. As you know I was out of business as a writer except for 6 earlier pieces and the poems (where I tried to distill what I never knew if I would get to write) from early 1942 through 1945.

Charles Hamilton Auction Number 56 (*1972*), #*146.*

Château-Thierry. It is possible that Fitzgerald may have made a suggestion about the Marines in conversation; but it is not in his memo. Perkins also felt that Hemingway should re-introduce the war at the end of the novel to combine the themes of love and war. He wrote on 24 May: "Still, I can't shake off the feeling that war, which has deeply conditioned this love story—and does so still passively—should still do so actively and decisively."

Although Hemingway later insisted that he had rejected Fitzgerald's advice on *A Farewell to Arms,* he did act on the recommendation to cut Frederic Henry's cosmic ruminations at the opening of Chapter 40 (typescript pages 293–294):

We had a fine life; all the things we did were of no importance and the things we said were foolish and seem even more idiotic to write down but we were happy and I suppose wisdom and happiness do not go together, although there is a wisdom in being a fool that we do not know much about and if happiness is an end sought by the wise it is no less an end if it comes without wisdom. It is as well to seize it as to seek it because you are liable to wear out the capacity for it in the seeking. To seek it through the kingdom of Heaven is a fine thing but you must give up this life first and if this life is all you have you might have remorse after giving it up and the kingdom of heaven might be a cold place in which to live with remorse. They say the only way you can keep a thing is to lose it and this may be true but I do not admire it. The only thing I know is that if you love anything enough they take it away from you. This may all be done in infinite wisdom but whoever does it is not my friend. I am afraid of God at night but I would have admired him more if he would have stopped the war or never let it start. Maybe he did stop it but whoever stopped it did not do it prettily. And if it is the Lord that giveth and the Lord that taketh away I do not admire him for taking Catherine away. He may have given me Catherine but who gave Rinaldi the syphillis at about the same time? The one thing I know is that I don't know anything about it. I see the wisdom of the priest at our mess who has always loved God and so is happy and I am sure that nothing will ever take God away from him. But how much is wisdom and how much is luck to be born that way? And what if you are not built that way? What if the things you love are perishable? All you know then is that they will perish. You will perish too and perhaps that is the answer; that those who love things that are immortal and believe in them are immortal themselves and live on with them while those that love things that die and believe in them die and are as dead as the things they love. If that were true it would be a fine gift and would even things up. But it probably is not true. All that we can be sure of is that we are born and that we will die and that everything we love will die too. The more things with life that we love the more things there are to die. So if we want to buy winning tickets we can go over on the side of immortality; and finally they most of them do. But if you were born loving nothing and the warm milk of your mother's breast

[85]

was never heaven and the first thing you loved was the side of a hill and the last thing was a woman and they took her away and you did not want another but only to have her; and she was gone; then you are not so well placed and it would have been better to have loved God from the start. But you did not love God. And it doesn't do any good to talk about it either. Nor to think about it.

This windy passage weakens the conclusion of the novel by announcing Catherine's impending death.

Fitzgerald was unhappy with the original ending:

> There are a great many more details, starting with my first meeting with an undertaker, and all the business of burial in a foreign country and going on with the rest of my life—which has gone on and seems likely to go on for a long time.
>
> I could tell how Rinaldi was cured of the syphilis and lived to find that the technic learned in wartime surgery is not of much practial use in peace. I could tell how the priest in our mess lived to be a priest in Italy under Fascism. I could tell how Ettore became a Fascist and the part he took in that organization. I could tell how Piani got to be a taxi–driver in New York and what sort of a singer Simmons became. Many things have happened. Everything blunts and the world keeps on. It never stops. It only stops for you. Some of it stops while you are still alive. The rest goes on and you go with it.
>
> I could tell you what I have done since March, nineteen hundred and eighteen, when I walked that night in the rain back to the hotel where Catherine and I had lived and went upstairs to our room and undressed and slept finally, because I was so tired—to wake in the morning with the sun shining in the window; then suddenly to realize what had happened. I could tell you what has happened since then, but that is the end of the story.

Hemingway tried out Fitzgerald's advice to replace this groping material with Frederic Henry's soliloquy from Chapter 34: "If people bring so much courage to this world the world has to kill them to break them, so of course it kills them. The world breaks every one and afterward many are strong at the broken places. But those that will not break it kills. It kills the very good and the very gentle and the very brave impartially. If you are none of these you can be sure it will kill you too but there will be no special hurry." Hemingway renumbered this page and inserted it in the typescript as the conclusion, but then changed his mind and restored it to its original position. Fitzgerald's admiration for this passage is attested by Callaghan, who visited him while he was reading the typescript of *A Farewell to Arms*. Fitzgerald read the passage aloud with emotion. When Callaghan expressed the reservation that it was perhaps "too deliberate," Fitzgerald was offended and began needling him about what it took to impress him. Finally he tried to stand on his head, asking if that would impress Callaghan.

There are thirty-five drafts for the ending of *A Farewell to Arms* among Hemingway's papers. He finally wrote the published version with its controlled understatement:

> Outside the room, in the hall, I spoke to the doctor, "is there anything I can do to-night?"
>
> "No. There is nothing to do. Can I take you to your hotel?"
>
> "No, thank you. I am going to stay here a while."
>
> "I know there is nothing to say. I cannot tell you————"
>
> "No," I said. "There's nothing to say."
>
> "Good-night," he said. "I cannot take you to your hotel?"
>
> "No, thank you."
>
> "It was the only thing to do," he said. "The operation proved————"
>
> "I do not want to talk about it," I said.
>
> "I would like to take you to your hotel."
>
> "No, thank you."
>
> He went down the hall. I went to the door of the room.
>
> "You can't come in now," one of the nurses said.
>
> "Yes I can," I said.
>
> "You can't come in yet."
>
> "You get out," I said. "The other one too."
>
> But after I had got them out and shut the door and turned off the light it wasn't any good. It was like saying good-by to a statue. After a while I went out and left the hospital and walked back to the hotel in the rain.

Morley Callaghan.

June 1929 brought another strain on the vulnerable friendship between Fitzgerald and Hemingway, but the consequences were delayed. Hemingway had been boxing regularly in Paris with Morley Callaghan, whom he had known on the *Toronto Star*. Although Callaghan was four inches shorter than Hemingway, he had quick hands and was more than able to hold his own. Callaghan is one of the experienced boxers who have testified that Hemingway was a clumsy boxer. During one of their bouts Callaghan cut Hemingway's mouth, and was dumfounded when Hemingway spat a mouthful of blood in his face. Hemingway explained that this was a bullfighter's way of expressing contempt for an injury.

Fitzgerald knew about these boxing bouts and was eager to see them. Hemingway finally invited him to come along as timekeeper. Here is Callaghan's account published thirty-four years later in *That Summer in Paris:*

> On the way to the American Club in a taxi, it seemed to me that Scott and Ernest were at ease with each other. . . . Then Ernest had him take out his watch and gave him his instructions. A round was to be three minutes, then a minute for rest. As he took these instructions, listening carefully, Scott had none of Miró's air of high professionalism. He was too enchanted at being there with us. Moving off the bench, he

squatted down, a little smile on his face. "Time," he called.

Our first round was like most of the rounds we had fought that summer, with me shuffling around, and Ernest, familiar with my style, leading and chasing after me. No longer did he rush in with his old brisk confidence. Now he kept an eye on my left and he was harder to hit. . . .

"Time," Scott called promptly. When we sat down beside him, he was rather quiet, meditative, and I could tell by the expression on his face that he was mystified. He must have come there with some kind of a picture of Ernest, the fighter, in his head. For Ernest and me it was just like any other day. We chatted and laughed. And it didn't seem to be important to us that Scott was there. He had made no comment that could bother us. He seemed to be content that he was there concentrating on the minute hand of his watch. "Time," he called.

Right at the beginning of that round Ernest got careless; he came in too fast, his left down, and he got smacked on the mouth. His lip began to bleed. It had often happened. It should have meant nothing to him. Hadn't he joked with Jimmy, the bartender, about always having me for a friend while I could make his lip bleed? Out of the corner of his eye he may have seen the shocked expression on Scott's face. Or the taste of blood in his mouth may have made him want to fight more savagely. He came lunging in, swinging more reck-lessly. As I circled around him, I kept jabbing at his bleeding mouth. I had to forget all about Scott, for Ernest had become rougher, his punching a little wilder than usual. His heavy punches, if they had landed, would have stunned me. I had to punch faster and harder myself to keep away from him. It bothered me that he was taking the punches on the face like a man telling himself he only needed to land one big punch himself.

. . . I was wondering why I was tiring, for I hadn't been hit solidly. Then Ernest, wiping the blood from his mouth with his glove, and probably made careless with exasperation and embarrassment from having Scott there, came leaping in at me. Stepping in, I beat him to the punch. The timing must have been just right. I caught him on the jaw; spinning around he went down, sprawled out on his back.

If Ernest and I had been there alone I would have

[89]

laughed. I was sure of my boxing friendship with him; in a sense I was sure of him, too. Ridiculous things had happened in that room. Hadn't he spat in my face? And I felt no surprise seeing him flat on his back. Shaking his head a little to clear it, he rested a moment on his back. As he rose slowly, I expected him to curse, then laugh.

"Oh, my God!" Scott cried suddenly. When I looked at him, alarmed, he was shaking his head helplessly. "I let the round go four minutes," he said.

"Christ!" Ernest yelled. He got up. He was silent a few seconds. Scott, staring at his watch, was mute and wondering. I wished I were miles away. "All right, Scott," Ernest said savagely, "if you want to see me getting the shit knocked out of me, just say so. Only don't say you made a mistake," and he stomped off to the shower room to wipe the blood from his mouth.

As I tried to grasp the meaning behind his fierce words I felt helpless with wonder, and nervous too; I seemed to be on the edge of some dark pit, and I could only stare blankly at Scott, who, as his eyes met mine, looked sick. Ernest had told me he had been avoiding Scott because Scott was a drunk and a nuisance and he didn't want to be bothered with him. It was plain now it wasn't the whole story. Lashing out with those bitter angry words, Ernest had practically shouted that he was aware Scott had some deep hidden animosity toward him. Shaken as I was, it flashed through my mind, Is the animosity in Scott, or is it really in Ernest? And why should it be in Ernest? Did Scott do something for him once? Is it that Scott helped him along and for months and months he's wanted to be free of him? Or does he think he knows something—knows Scott has to resent him? What is it? Not just that Scott's a drunk. I knew there was something else.

Then Scott came over to me, his face ashen, and he whispered, "Don't you see I got fascinated watching? I forgot all about the watch. My God, he thinks I did it on purpose. Why would I do it on purpose?"

"You wouldn't," I said, deeply moved, for he looked so stricken. For weeks he had been heaping his admiration of Ernest on me, his hero worship, and I knew of his eagerness for the companionship. Anyone who could say that he was under some secret and malevolent compulsion to let the round go on would have to say, too, that all men are twisted and no man knows what is in his heart. All I knew was that for weeks he had wanted to be here with us, and now that he was here it had brought him this.

"Look, Scott," I whispered. "If you did it on purpose you wouldn't have suddenly cried out that you had let the round go on. You didn't need to. You would have kept quiet. Ernest will see it himself." But Scott didn't answer. . . . The anguish in his face was the anguish of a man who felt that everything he had stood for when he had been at his best, had been belittled.

"Come on, Scott," I whispered. "Ernest didn't mean it. It's a thing I might have said myself. A guy gets sore and blurts out the first crazy thing that comes into his head."

"No, you heard him. He believes I did it on purpose," he whispered bitterly. "What can I do, Morley?"

"Don't do anything," I whispered. "Forget the whole thing. He'll want to forget it himself. You'll see."

He moved away from me as Ernest returned from the shower room. With his face washed, Ernest looked much calmer. He had probably done a lot of thinking, too. Yet he offered no retraction. For my part, I tried to ignore the whole incident. Since we had had a good two or three minutes' rest to make up for the long round, why couldn't we go on now? I asked. It gave us something to do. Ernest and I squared off.

Scott, appearing alert and efficient, and hiding his terrible sense of insult and bitterness, called "Time." As I look back now I wonder why it didn't occur to me, as we began the round, that Ernest might try to kill me. But between us there was no hostility. The fact that I had been popping him, and then had clipped him and knocked him down, was part of our boxing. We went a good brisk round, both keeping out of trouble. When we clinched, my eye would wander to Scott, sitting there so white-faced. Poor Scott. Then suddenly he made it worse. The corner of a wrestling mat stuck out from under the parallel bars, and when I half tripped on it and went down on one knee, Scott, to mollify Ernest, called out foolishly, but eagerly, "One knockdown to Ernest, one to Morley," and if I had been Ernest I think I would have snarled at him, no matter how good his intentions were.

[91]

The mood of the afternoon was changed to the ridiculous when a young fellow who had been watching the boxing offered Hemingway some advice and made himself foolish.

> The student's absurd intervention, adding to the general sense of humiliation, must have put Scott more on edge. He must have felt bewildered. Yet now my two friends began to behave splendidly. Not a word was said about the student. We were all suddenly polite, agreeable, friendly and talkative. I knew how Scott felt; he had told me. He felt bitter, insulted, disillusioned in the sense that he had been aware of an antagonism in Ernest. Only one thing could have saved him for Ernest. An apology. A restoration of respect, a lifting of the accusation. But Ernest had no intention of apologizing. He obviously saw no reason why he should. So we all behaved splendidly. We struck up graceful camaraderie. Ernest was jovial with Scott. We were all jovial. We went out and walked up to the Falstaff. And no one watching us sitting at the bar could have imagined that Scott's pride had been shattered.

On 28 August 1929 Hemingway sent Perkins a report of the bout from Spain, which differs from Callaghan's recollection. According to Hemingway, he, Fitzgerald, and John Peale Bishop had eaten a winey lunch of lobster thermidor at Prunier's. Feeling sleepy, Ernest decided to box with Callaghan right away instead of later in the afternoon as arranged and had a couple of whiskeys on the way. Because of his dull condition, Ernest stipulated one-minute rounds with two-minute rests. Callaghan hit him freely but did not knock him down. Ernest "slipped and went down once and lit on my arm and put my left shoulder out in that first round and it pulled a tendon so that it was pretty sore afterwards." If Callaghan could hit hard, he "would have killed me." Ernest sensed that the round was going long but couldn't ask Scott because then Callaghan would have thought he was quitting. Scott finally called time and apologized for letting the round go three minutes and 45 seconds. They boxed five more rounds. Hemingway's letter to Perkins is controlled and does not express any anger at Fitzgerald.

In 1951 Hemingway sent Arthur Mizener a detailed account of that afternoon in June 1929. In this version the rounds were supposed to be two minutes long with one-minute rests; but Scott let the first round go thirteen minutes, during which Callaghan was hitting Ernest freely for eight minutes but could not knock him down. When Scott finally called time, Ernest said he was a son-of-a-bitch for deliberately letting the round go thirteen minutes. In the first long round Callaghan had punched himself out, so Ernest was pretty sure he could knock him out in the later rounds; but he did not want to, even though Callaghan had tried to knock him out. One detail in Hemingway's letter to Mizener that merits comment is his claim that Fitzgerald let the first round go thirteen minutes—a very long time in the ring. Rounds in professional fights are three minutes long.

For the time being the matter of the long round was dropped. Shortly afterward, the Hemingways went to Spain for the bullfights and Fitzgerald went to the Riviera to work on his novel. In July Hemingway wrote Fitzgerald from Valencia about the seizure of the June *Scribner's Magazine* in Boston because of the second installment of *A Farewell to Arms,* expressing concern about the possible effect on Scribners' attitude toward publication of the book. He signed himself "E. Cantwork Hemingstein." Fitzgerald replied reassuringly:

> 12 Blvd. Eugene Gazagnaire
> Cannes,
> Aug 23d 1929
>
> Dear Ernest:
> I've been working like hell, better than for four years, + now am confident of getting old faithful off before the all-American teams are picked—hence the delay.
> I wrote Max (not mentioning your letter) one of these don't-lose-your-head notes, though I, like you, never thot there was more than an outside chance of his being forced to let you down. I felt sure that if it came to a crisis he'd threaten to resign + force their hand.
> The book sticks with me, by the way; I'm sure its all I thought at first + can't wait to read it in printing letters.
> Its been gay here but we are, thank God, desperately unpopular + not invited anywhere. See the Murphys once a week or so—Gerald is older, less gay, more social, but not

so changed as many people in five years. D. Parker is on the crest—tho I didn't see her as much as I'd liked.

Now—Ruth Goldbeck Voallammbbrrossa[34] not only had no intention of throwing you out in any case, but has even promised *on her own initiative* to speak to whoever it is—she knows her—has the place. She is a fine woman, I think; one of the most attractive in evidence at this moment, in every sense, + is not deserving of that nervous bitterness.

Not knowing whether you've left Spain I'm sending this to Paris. Hoping you'll be here in Sept for a week or so.

Bunny Wilson's book [*I Thought of Daisy*] has a facinating portrait of Dos [John Dos Passo] in it, + is full of good things, + to me interesting throughout. Oddly enough what it lacks is his old bogey, form. It is shapeless as Wells at his wildest, or almost.

Have read nothing good recently save a book on the Leopold Loeb case + Harold Nicolson's Tennyson, neither recent.

This is a dull letter but it's late + what's left of the mind is tired

Always Afftly Yrs

Scott

Best to Pauline.

During the summer of 1929 Fitzgerald wrote "The Swimmers," a *Saturday Evening Post* story in which he obliquely commented on the term "lost generation" that had been given currency by *The Sun Also Rises*. Hemingway's novel had two epigraphs: one from *Ecclesiastes* describing the order of nature ("the earth abideth forever"); and one from Gertrude Stein ("You are all a lost generation"). Stein had reported to Hemingway this comment by a French garage owner about his young mechanic. The Stein statement was picked up by most readers as the key to *The Sun Also Rises*. It was generally assumed that the novel proclaimed the existence of a lost generation of war casualties—and that, moreover, Heming-

---

34 The Hemingways were subletting an apartment from Ruth Obre-Goldbeck-de Vallombrosa.

way identified with them. Years later the author corrected this impression, explaining that the Stein epigraph was meant ironically or sarcastically. In *A Moveable Feast,* he wrote, "But the hell with her lost-generation talk and all the dirty, easy labels." "The Swimmers" was an attempt to express Fitzgerald's feelings about the values of France and America, and it became a patriotic hymn. At the end of this story an American who is returning to France broods about the promises of America: "There was a lost generation in the saddle at the moment, but it seemed to him that the men coming on, the men of the war, were better; and all his old feeling that America was a bizarre accident, a sort of historical sport, had gone forever. The best of America was the best of the world." Here Fitzgerald categorizes as a lost generation those men who had been too old for the war, placing his hope in the idealistic younger men who had fought in the Great War.

Hemingway wrote from Madrid on 4 September urging Fitzgerald to stick with his novel, saying that the parts he had read were better than anything except the best part of *The Great Gatsby.* Ernest repeats his charge that Scott had been constipated by Gilbert Seldes' review of *Gatsby* because it made him try for a masterpiece. Only fairies deliberately write masterpieces. Other writers just write as well as they can. If Seldes hadn't made him self-conscious, Scott would have finished two good novels by now.

Hemingway's letter produced a reply from Fitzgerald on 9 September which is a mixture of the self-defense and the self-abnegation that would characterize much of his subsequent correspondence with Hemingway.

> Villa Fleur des Bois
> Cannes. Sept 9th 1929

Dear Ernest:

I'm glad you decided my letter wasn't snooty—it was merely hurried (incidently I thought you wanted a word said to Ruth G. if it came about naturally—I merely remarked that you'd be disappointed if you lost your appartment—never a word that you'd been exasperated.) But enough of pretty dismal matters—let us proceed to the really dismal ones. First tho let me say that from Perkins last your book like Pickwick has become a classic while still in serial form. Everything looks bright as day for it and I envy you like hell but would rather have it happen to you than to anyone else.

Just taken another chapter to typists + its left me in a terrible mood of depression as to whether its any good or not. In 2½ mos. I've been here I've written 20,000 words on it + one short story, which is suberb for me of late years. I've paid for it with the usual nervous depressions and such drinking manners as the lowest bistrop bistrot?) boy would scorn. My latest tendency is to collapse about 11.00 and, with the tears flowing from my eyes or the gin rising to their level and leaking over, + tell interested friends or acquaintances that I havn't a friend in the world and likewise care for nobody, generally including Zelda, and often implying current company—after which the current company tend to become less current and I wake up in strange rooms in strange palaces. The rest of the time I stay alone working or trying to work or brooding or reading detective stories—and realizing that anyone in my state of mind who has in addition never been able to hold his tongue, is pretty poor company. But when drunk I make them all pay and pay and pay.

Among them has been Dotty Parker. Naturally she having been in an equivalent state lacks patience—(this isn't snooty—no one likes to see people in moods of despair they themselves have survived.) incidently the Murphys have given their whole performance for her this summer and I think, tho she would be the last to admit it, she's had the time of her life.

We're coming to Paris for 2 mos the 1st of October.

Your analysis of my inability to get my serious work done is too kind in that it leaves out dissipation, but among acts of God it is possible that the 5 yrs between my leaving the army + finishing *Gatsby* 1919–1924 which included 3 novels, about 50 popular stories + a play + numerous articles + movies may have taken all I had to say too early, adding that all the time we were living at top speed in the gayest worlds we could find. This *au fond* is what really worries me—tho the trouble may be my inability to leave anything once started. I have worked for

2 months over a popular short story that was foredoomed
to being torn up when completed. Perhaps the house will
burn down with this ms + preferably me in it
                    Always Your Stinking Old Friend
                                        Scott
I have no possible right to send you this gloomy letter.
Really if I didn't feel rather better with one thing or another I couldn't have written it. Here's a last flicker of the
old cheap pride:—the *Post* now pays the old whore $4,000.
a screw. But now it's because she's mastered the 40 posi-
tions—in her youth one was enough.

Even though Fitzgerald had been unable to complete his novel,
he was a hard-working writer. In his first decade as a professional
writer (1919–1928) he published three novels, three collections of
stories, and a play. His short-story and article output in this period
topped one hundred. That he squandered his talent on popular
short stories to make the money that he squandered is undeniable.
Nonetheless, the stereotypical view of Fitzgerald as a writer who
did not work hard is false. He was at least as productive as Hemingway. In his first decade as a non-journalistic professional (1923–
1932) Hemingway published two pamphlets, two novels, one parody, two volumes of stories, and a nonfiction study of the bullfight;
his total of published stories and articles in this ten-year period was
twenty-five. The crucial difference was in the public images Fitzgerald and Hemingway projected. Hemingway radiated confidence
and dedication. Everything he did seemed related to his work.
Fitzgerald, who had an abysmal sense of literary public relations,
became a symbol for dissipation and irresponsibility. As Hemingway recognized, at some point in the late Nineteen-Twenties, Fitzgerald seemed to enjoy failure. Perhaps it was a function of what
Fitzgerald called his "Puritan conscience developed in Minnesota"
to humiliate him for his failure to fulfill his ambitions. He knew
how good he was: geniuses always know.

Hemingway replied on 13 September with a warm and encouraging letter. He says that Scott has more ability and more concern about his own work than anyone, and pleads with him not to
interrupt the novel to write stories. Ernest picks up on Scott's

reference to himself as an "old whore," explaining that Scott is not an old whore because an old whore's price is never raised. Scott's stories are not whore-work, but they are bad judgment. He should be able to give them up and live on the earnings of his novels. Writers get better, Ernest insists, after they lose their first bloom because they develop métier and know how to use it. The only thing to do with a novel is to keep writing until it's finished. Ernest repeats his wish that Scott's income could depend on novels instead of the damned stories.

One reason why Fitzgerald could not live on his novels was that they were not best sellers. The total earnings from book sales for the three novels during 1920–1926 was $37,000—an average of $5300 a year. Exclusive of dramatic and serial rights, *This Side of Paradise* brought $14,200, *The Beautiful and Damned* $15,900, and *The Great Gatsby* $6700. Moreover, the interval of eight years between *Gatsby* and *Tender Is the Night* was not extraordinary, except for the circumstance that Fitzgerald was trying to finish the novel during much of this period. Eight years elapsed between *A Farewell to Arms* and *To Have and Have Not,* which was pieced together from short stories; and there was an eleven-year interval between *A Farewell to Arms* and *For Whom the Bell Tolls.*

After serialization in *Scribner's Magazine, A Farewell to Arms* was published on 27 September 1929 and was an immediate success with readers and reviewers. In *The Nation* Clifton Fadiman called it "a real occasion for patriotic rejoicing." The first printing of 31,050 copies sold fast; two more printings were required in September, one in October, and three more in November. By February 1930 more than 79,000 copies had been sold—which earned the author at least $30,000 in book royalties. Hemingway later claimed that sales were hurt because the novel appeared on the day of the stock-market crash, but the crash occurred on 29 October—a month later. Fitzgerald's total income for 1929 was $32,448.18—of which $27,000 came from stories and $31.71 from all of his books.

In October Fitzgerald passed on to Hemingway a letter from Harold Ober, who had left Reynolds and set up his own literary agency, explaining to Fitzgerald that Reynolds had tried to place Hemingway's stories without consulting Ober. Fitzgerald added a marginal note:

As you'll see from this, while Ober was simply wondering if you wanted to use him Reynolds went ahead + constituted himself your agent, though as his only approach to you was through me, he was stepping forth. Of course this letter is nothing but Ober being sore and your work is financially safe with Reynolds as long as he doesn't go senile. I simply pass this on to show how the battle over your work increases in speed now that you don't need any help. In any case I shall step out here, not even answering this letter except in the vaguest terms I liked Cowly's review in Sun. Tribune. First intelligent one I've seen

Scott

In the fall of 1929 Fitzgerald and Hemingway were again in Paris, and Gertrude Stein asked Hemingway to bring Fitzgerald to call. Hemingway's note relaying the invitation mentions that she says Scott is the most talented writer of his generation. Stein generated a small crisis by repeating this judgment to Ernest and Scott—adding that Scott's "flame" was stronger than Ernest's. It is not clear why Fitzgerald was so upset by Stein's remark, but he seems to have felt that she didn't mean it and was somehow slighting him or Hemingway or both. Hemingway appears in an attractive role as he sends Fitzgerald a four-page holograph letter patiently explaining that Stein's compliment was sincere. He swears that Stein has never said anything to him about Scott that wasn't praise. Ernest does not feel that he is competing with Scott. Stein meant that Scott has more natural talent than he does, and she believes that Scott's talent is of a better quality. All talk about "flames" is horseshit, and comparison of Scott and Ernest is worthless because their work has nothing in common. Ernest has no feelings of superiority or inferiority to Scott. There shouldn't be such feelings between writers who are all in the same boat headed for death. The only competition a writer should feel is the internal one to write well. Ernest understands that Scott is touchy because he hasn't finished his novel, and it wouldn't bother him if Scott were even touchier.

The delayed reactions to the June Hemingway-Callaghan bout occurred in November 1929 when reports appeared in American newspapers. On the 24th Isabel M. Paterson's "Turns With a

Bookworm" column in the *New York Herald Tribune* printed this incorrect, troublemaking item:

> In "The Denver Post" Caroline Bancroft tells an amusing story of a singular encounter between Ernest Hemingway and Morley Callaghan.
>
> "One night at the Dome Callaghan's name was mentioned and Hemingway said: 'Oh, you can easily see he hasn't any practical background for his fight stories—shouldn't think he knew anything about boxing.'. . . Callaghan, hearing of it, challenged Hemingway. . . . After arranging for rounds and a considerable audience, they entered the arena. Not many seconds afterward Callaghan knocked Hemingway out cold. The amateur timekeeper was so excited he forgot to count and the deflated critic had to stagger up and finish the round. When last seen Callaghan was demanding a bout with Jim Tully, saying that he wants to take on all the rough boys of literature."

Callaghan saw the article in Toronto and, hoping to undo the mischief before Hemingway heard about it, sent a correction to Paterson on the 26th of November. His letter was published in the *Trib* on the 8th of December.

> Last Saturday I saw the story of the singular encounter between Ernest Hemingway and me, taken from the Denver Post. It is a fine story and you can imagine how much I regret not deserving such a reputation, but this ought to be said:
>
> Hemingway, as far as I know, never sat at the Dome last summer.
>
> Certainly he never sat there panning my fight stories and whatever background I might have for them.
>
> I have only written one fight story anyway. I'll have to do some more at once.
>
> Nor did I ever challenge Hemingway.
>
> Eight or nine times we went boxing last summer trying to work up a sweat, and an increased eagerness for an extra glass of beer afterwards. We never had an audience.
>
> Nor did I ever knock out Hemingway. Once we had a timekeeper. If there was any kind of a remarkable performance that afternoon the timekeeper deserved the applause.

Being of a peaceful and shy disposition I have only envy for strong men who challenge each other and then knock each other out. But I do wish you'd correct that story or I'll never be able to go to New York again for fear of getting knocked about.

Callaghan had a clear understanding of how Hemingway would react to any public disparagement of his boxing reputation and tried to cover himself by sending a copy of his *Trib* letter to Perkins on 6 December, explaining that he hadn't sent it to Perkins before because he knew Perkins would see it when the *Trib* printed it. But now Callaghan is angry because he has just received a cable from Fitzgerald which places the onus of the story on him. Callaghan says the story was current in New York before he left Paris and that he told only three people in Paris about boxing with Hemingway. He never spoke to anyone from the *Denver Post*. Callaghan asks Perkins to tell Hemingway that the story did not come from him. It is noteworthy that Callaghan did not write directly to Hemingway. Perkins replied on 9 December: "I won't write to Ernest unless he sometime raises the point, because I think that would be a mistake;—but I shall write Scott and through him it will get to Ernest."

Before his letter was printed in the *Trib,* Callaghan received a collect cable from Paris: HAVE SEEN STORY IN HERALD TRIBUNE. ERNEST AND I AWAIT YOUR CORRECTION. SCOTT FITZGERALD. Callaghan did not know that Hemingway had pressured Fitzgerald to send the cable, and he reacted with an angry letter to Fitzgerald: "I told him it had been unnecessary for him to rush in to defend Ernest. For him to hurry out and send that cable to me collect without waiting to see what I would do was the act of a son of a bitch and I could only assume that he was drunk as usual when he sent it."[35]

35 Allen Tate was in Paris at the time; his recollection of the events surrounding the Callaghan-Hemingway bout demonstrates how difficult it is to establish the truth about virtually everything involving Hemingway: "In a few seconds Ernest was lying flat on his back. Callaghan had knocked him out. Callaghan rushed straight to the shower, put on his clothes, and rushed to the nearest poste et telegraphe and sent a cable to his publisher: 'Just knocked out Ernest Hemingway.' Well, Ernest made Scott cable Max Perkins at Scribners denying the whole thing. Scott went on a drunk that lasted three weeks. He'd come around and say, 'What a son of a bitch I was to tell that lie' " ("Interview with Allen Tate," *Fitzgerald/Hemingway Annual* 1974). No such cables from Callaghan or Fitzgerald to Perkins exist.

It is possible that this matter could have been de-escalated if the parties had not been communicating by transatlantic ship mail; but Hemingway was also angry with Callaghan for repeating Robert McAlmon's gossip. The rumor about a homosexual relationship between Fitzgerald and Hemingway was spread by McAlmon, who was himself bisexual and had a malicious mouth. In October 1929 Perkins informed Fitzgerald that McAlmon was in New York slandering Hemingway "both as a man and as a writer." Fitzgerald explained to Perkins on 15 November: "Part of his quarrel with Ernest some years ago was because he assured Ernest that I was a fairy—God knows he shows more creative imagination in his malice than in his work. Next he told Callaghan that Ernest was a fairy." On 10 December Hemingway wrote Perkins that Fitzgerald came to dinner last night and while drunk said that Perkins had written that McAlmon had slandered Hemingway in New York. Scott reported a filthy story about himself and Ernest that Callaghan had heard from McAlmon. Ernest knows that McAlmon had said that Pauline is a Lesbian, that Ernest is a fairy, and that Ernest caused the premature birth of Bumby by beating Hadley. Now Callaghan is spreading the story of Ernest's homosexuality—along with the story of how Callaghan knocked him out. Ernest will have to administer beatings to McAlmon and Callaghan. He tells Perkins not to blame Scott for violating a confidence because he is completely honorable when sober but irresponsible when drunk.

Fitzgerald came to feel that McAlmon's gossip about him and Hemingway contributed to the destruction of the friendship. He commented in his *Notebooks:* "I really loved him, but of course it wore out like a love affair. The fairies have spoiled all that." Hemingway is not named, but the reference is clear.

McAlmon's gossip led to punitive action by Hemingway, as recorded in a previously unpublished letter by James Charters (Jimmy the Barman), a popular Paris figure:

As I got within a few steps of the entrance to the bar I recognized Ernest Hemingway from behind. Hemingway didn't see or hear me behind him. He was also with another gentleman, whos face I didn't see. Well now only about three feet away and on a line with Hemingway and his friend was Bob

McAlmon. All three making for my bar. Suddenly before I could do anything, Hemingway sent accross a lightening right swing to Bob McAlmons chin saying at the same time. *Now tell that to your God-damn friends!* which I distinctly heard. Though Bob didn't fall with the blow for the wall of the bar in the street protected him he began bleeding from a cut from the lower part of his mouth and chin. Then as Hemingway and his friend moved into the bar I at the same time rushed over to Bob to help him into the bar where I got the proprietors wife to wash and bathe the wound and give him a clean handkerchief to hold to his face until the cut dried. Well it was a most embarrassing situation I'd been in for some time. Bob McAlmon has he received the unexpected blow, and without saying anything, looked straight at me very appealingly. At the same time Hemingway not expecting me to have shown up and saw what happened gazed at me rather surprised and somewhat embarrassed. He didn't speak either. Though I got both his and Bob McAlmons message from the expressions on each of their faces. Silence appeared to be the general key-note. I myself couldn't possibly take sides as they were both very good clients, and friends of mine. I really had to be at my most tactful best right to the end of that unfortunate affaire. Inside has Bob stood by the bar holding the new handkerchief to his face, everyone there appeared on edge. First all eyes where on Bob McAlmon, then onto Hemingway, and his friend, who where sitting at a small round table by the entrance. I'd already served them a scotch each which Ernest whispered to me to bring along. However after getting Bob to drink a good shot of brandy he seemed to feel, and looked much better I then asked him if he would like to go home to his hotel for the night and should I get him a taxi. He said yes. So when the taxi arrived Bob gave me his address to give the driver. At the same time I mentioned to the driver that his passenger had just had an accident, and so would he please see him safely home. With that I bid both Bob and the driver good night, and returned to the bar. Just then Hemingway made a sign in mime for two more Scotchs. Well now I recognized Hemingway's friend but pretended not to have done. For as we hadn't seen each other since the early 20s at the Dingo both he and Hemingway were hoping I didn't recognize him. It was Scott Fitzgerald. Fitzgerald kept silent

[103]

all the way through at least within my close hearing or anyone elses in the bar who might understand what was said I also was waiting for Hemingway to tell me who his friend was, but this happened never. Ernest ordered the drinks and paid for them, so I had no reason to go to Scott, except to serve him his drinks. I gathered that Hemingway by keeping down to a minimum what might become a barroom scandal involving several famous people if the news leaked out. Scott Fitzgerald was completely protected by remaining quiet, not getting involver, or taking sides. Hemingway began talking to me as I stood by his side. Never once did he bring up the trouble between him and Bob McAlmon, but switched to asking me if I liked and was satisfied with the introduction he wrote for the Paris memoires. *This Must Be The Place*[36]

Jimmy's letter—written in 1973—places this scene in a bar off the Boulevard Montparnasse "around 1932–33." If so, then Fitzgerald could not have been present because the Fitzgeralds left Europe permanently in September 1931; moreover, Jimmy's recognition of Fitzgerald seems rather shaky. If it happened in 1933 (Hemingway's introduction to *This Must Be the Place* was sent from Africa in 1933), then Fitzgerald was not there. If Fitzgerald was there, then it happened before September 1931. The beating almost certainly occurred, but it is highly unlikely that Fitzgerald was present.

About the 11th of December 1929—before the 8 December *Trib* reached Europe—Hemingway wrote Fitzgerald a five-page holograph letter absolving him of all blame for his timekeeping blunder. Again this letter shows Hemingway in a highly favorable light, trying to save a friendship by admitting his own character faults. He denies having said that Scott was guilty of bad timekeeping and is sure that Scott did not do it deliberately. He knows that Scott is a man of great honor whereas he is not—at least not in boxing. When he boxed with Jean Prévost he arranged with the timekeeper to call time whenever he was in trouble but to let the round go on if he was hitting Prévost. Two of Ernest's friends have died recently and he won't allow his friendship with Scott to be ruined by this squabble. When they had talked about the time-

36 Charters to M.J.B., 5 August 1973.

keeping after the boxing, Ernest did not ask whether Scott had deliberately let the round continue until Scott admitted that he was trying to force a quarrel with him. Scott's remark that he felt a need to smash him caused Ernest to temporarily lapse into suspicion, but Ernest apologizes for that. He was upset at the time because he had just heard about the vile gossip of McAlmon and Callaghan. He wishes Scott didn't have such a bad reaction to alcohol, but he'll be okay when the novel is completed. Ernest insists that he had placed no importance on the boxing bout and had enjoyed telling people how Callaghan had hit him. He had gotten angry only after reading Callaghan's lies in the newspaper. Ernest reiterates that he holds Scott blameless. He values Scott's sense of honor and would never wound it.

On December 15 Hemingway wrote Perkins apologizing for bothering him about additional promotion for *A Farewell to Arms*, saying that Scott got him worried about continuing sales and had suggested that Scribners ought to advertise it as a love story. Ernest is fond of Scott, but he has been a trying friend. Scott is hard at work on his novel and will be all right when he finally finishes it.

Perkins tried to restore peace among Fitzgerald, Hemingway, and Callaghan; but his letter to Fitzgerald was not mailed until 17 December—and did not reach him until after Christmas:

> I am enclosing a letter I got from Callaghan, and a note which he sent to the Herald Tribune, and which was printed there. They will show you how things stand. The girl who started the story is one Caroline Bancroft. She wanders around Europe every year and picks up what she can in the way of gossip, and prints it in the Denver paper, and it spreads from there. Callaghan told me the whole story about boxing with Ernest, and the point he put the most emphasis on was your time-keeping. That impressed him a great deal. He did say that he knew he was more adept in boxing than Ernest, and that he had been practising for several years with fighters. He was all right about the whole matter. He is much better than he looks.

On 1 January 1930 Fitzgerald—having seen Callaghan's correction in the *Trib*—wrote to him in Toronto apologizing for his "stupid and hasty" cable.[37] He did not mean to imply that Callaghan had circulated the story. This letter did not reach Toronto until the 16th. Callaghan's conclusion that Fitzgerald's admiration for Hemingway had now been permanently destroyed is extremely dubious.

On the 4th of January Hemingway responded to the letter Callaghan had sent Fitzgerald in reply to the cable. After noting that Pierre Loving, a Paris journalist, had been responsible for the false report in the *Denver Post*,[38] he admits that Fitzgerald cabled Callaghan at his insistence—and against Scott's own judgment. Since three weeks had elapsed since the story appeared in print, Ernest had not known whether Callaghan had corrected it. But, if Callaghan would like to say about him what he wrote to Scott, Ernest will be in America soon and ready to meet him anywhere privately. Callaghan replied that he couldn't transfer his remarks about Fitzgerald to Hemingway. Since Ernest had forced Scott to send the cable, Callaghan would need a new set of epithets for Hemingway. Perkins, still trying to make peace, wrote Callaghan that Fitzgerald had tried to persuade Hemingway that the cable was unnecessary because Callaghan would promptly deny the story. Perkins assured Callaghan that he had behaved like a gentleman.

Callaghan reported to Perkins on 17 January that he has just received a letter from Scott apologizing for the cable. Scott writes that he never thought Callaghan started the false report, but felt that Callaghan should issue the denial from America. Callaghan asks Perkins to send Caroline Bancroft's letter to either Scott or Ernest. He is now rather sorry that he sent Scott the abusive letter, but Scott will probably understand why he wrote it.

On the 21st of January Fitzgerald replied to Perkins' 17 December letter: "Thank you for the documents in the Callaghan case. I'd rather not discuss it except to say that I don't like him and that I wrote him a formal letter of apology. I never thought he started the rumor + never said nor implied such a thing to Ernest."

Hemingway wrote to Callaghan on 21 February 1930 from Key West admitting that he had overreacted and explaining that he

37 This account is largely based on Callaghan's *That Summer in Paris;* the documents are in Mr. Callaghan's possession.
38 On 9 December 1929 Caroline Bancroft wrote Callaghan that her source for the boxing story was Virginia Hersch, who heard it in Paris.

had not intended to mail his 4 January letter—Pauline found it and mailed it. (This statement is supported by Hemingway's 10 January letter to Perkins asking him to intercept a letter to Callaghan sent c/o Scribners.) Hemingway insists that he could knock out Callaghan with small gloves, but suggests they call a truce. Callaghan replied that he doesn't think Hemingway could knock him out, but it is okay with him if Ernest believes it. He agrees to the armistice. Callaghan never heard from Fitzgerald or Hemingway again. When in 1947 Samuel Putnam's *Paris Was Our Mistress* included an anecdote about how Hemingway beat up Callaghan for defeating him at tennis, they both ignored it. Fitzgerald had been dead for seven years.

IV

In April 1930 Zelda Fitzgerald suffered a mental breakdown in Paris and was hospitalized in Switzerland until the fall of 1931, when the Fitzgeralds permanently returned to America. There is no surviving letter from Hemingway to Fitzgerald about Zelda's collapse. During his wife's hospitalization Fitzgerald's novel was again interrupted as he wrote short stories for ready money to pay medical bills. Hemingway divided his time between Key West and Wyoming in the hot months, with trips to Spain to gather material for *Death in the Afternoon*. The only located letter from this period is Hemingway's 12 April 1931 letter of condolence on the death of Fitzgerald's father, urging him to save his feelings about his father for a novel—and not to poop them away in *The Saturday Evening Post*.

Jay Allen, a reporter for the *Chicago Tribune,* met Hemingway in Madrid during the summer of 1931. After assuring Allen that he had graduated from Princeton, Hemingway sent a note by messenger explaining that he had lied because of his envy of Scott Fitzgerald's Princeton education.

Fitzgerald and Hemingway met in October of 1931, but the circumstances of the meeting are not known. Although he did not note it in his *Ledger,* the meeting is stipulated on the chart of their meetings that Fitzgerald later prepared (see below, p. 145). At this meeting Hemingway probably gave Fitzgerald his passport photo inscribed: "To Scott from his old bedfellow Richard Halliburton Princeton 1931." Halliburton was a Princetonian whose travel-adventure books were very popular. He was also an alleged homosexual. The photo shows a well-dressed Hemingway in a double-breasted suit, white shirt, and striped tie—but not a Guards tie. (Fitzgerald and Hemingway were both willing camera subjects, but no photo of them together is known.)

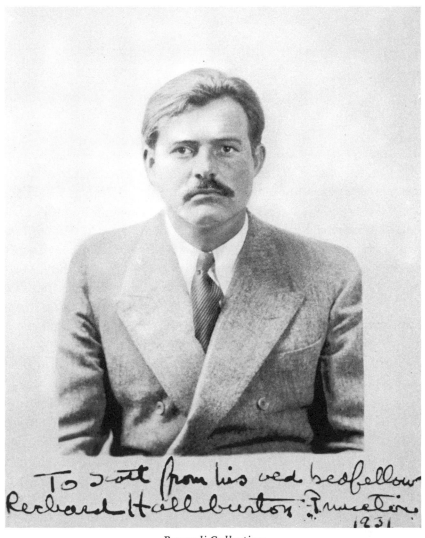

Bruccoli Collection.

Around this time Fitzgerald and Hemingway began relying on Perkins as a courier, relaying messages through him. Perkins tried to maintain the pretense that his two authors were still close friends, and his letters to each of them frequently included news about the other. The Fitzgeralds settled in Montgomery, Alabama, in the fall of 1931. In November–December Fitzgerald went alone to Hollywood to work on the screenplay for *Red-Headed Woman* at MGM. His screenplay was rejected; but he was paid $6,000, which he hoped would see him through his novel. On 9 December Hemingway wrote Perkins that he had not heard from Scott, except for a telegram from Hollywood recommending an agent to handle his movie rights. Beginning in 1932, Fitzgerald's comments about Hemingway to Perkins manifested increasing guilt about his own stalled career. In January 1932 he sent Perkins an optimistic progress report on his novel, adding: "Don't tell Ernest or anyone— let them think what they want—you're the only one whose ever consistently felt faith in me anyhow." Fitzgerald's work plans were again changed when Zelda suffered a relapse in February 1932. She was placed at the Phipps Clinic of Johns Hopkins Hospital, and in May Fitzgerald rented "La Paix" outside Baltimore to be near her. At Phipps, Zelda Fitzgerald wrote her novel, *Save Me the Waltz*, which Perkins accepted for publication. In May Fitzgerald warned Perkins about Hemingway's possible resentment of Zelda's novel:

> Now a second thing, more important than you think. You havn't been in the publishing business over twenty years without noticing the streaks of smallness in very large personalities. Ernest told me once he would "never publish a book in the same season with me", meaning it would lead to ill-feeling. I advise you, if he is in New York, (and always granting you like Zelda's book) *do not praise it, or even talk about it to him!* The finer the thing he has written [*Death in the Afternoon*], the more he'll expect your entire allegiance to it as this is one of the few pleasures, rich + full + new, he'll get out of it. I know this, + I think you do too. + probably there's no use warning you. There is no possible conflict between the books but there has always been a subtle struggle between Ernest + Zelda, + any apposition might have cureously grave

consequences—curious, that is, to un–jealous men like you and me.

In the summer of 1932 Perkins expressed to Hemingway the wild hope that Zelda could turn into a popular writer and take the financial pressure off Scott. Perkins and Fitzgerald have planned a tour of the Virginia Civil War battlefields and want Ernest to come along. Scott would like to join Perkins' next Key West fishing trip. Hemingway did not come to Virginia, and Fitzgerald never got to Key West. On the 27th of July Hemingway wrote Perkins that Scott should have traded Zelda in five or six years ago before she was certifiably crazy. "He is the great tragedy of talent in our bloody generation." Later the same day Hemingway sent Perkins a note apologizing for his brutality about "poor Scott," explaining that the Fitzgerald marriage always makes him bitter.

Death in the Afternoon, Hemingway's anatomy of tauromachy, was published on 23 September 1932. Hemingway sent Fitzgerald a copy, inscribed: "To Scott with much affection Ernest." The 10,300-copy first printing sold slowly. The Depression was blamed for the disappointing reception of this $3.50 volume, but it was not a book with much popular appeal at the time. Bullfighting did not yet have a large American following—although Hemingway would be largely responsible for later American interest in the spectacle. Zelda Fitzgerald's novel *Save Me the Waltz,* appeared on 7 October and fared less well. The 3000-copy first printing did not sell out. Reviewers and readers were put off by Zelda's extravagant style; and the Fitzgeralds were no longer newsworthy enough to generate interest in a roman à clef about their marriage. Perkins sent Hemingway a copy of *Save Me the Waltz,* which he acknowledged on 15 November, saying it is unreadable. He offers to give it to anyone Perkins thinks could read it.

Fitzgerald worked effectively on his novel at "La Paix" in 1932 and 1933. After replacing the matricide plot with the story of Dick Diver, he had material that was close to him and made steady progress. The deterioration of the brilliant psychiatrist drew heavily upon Fitzgerald's guilt about his own failure to fulfill his promise, his betrayal of his talent. While he was writing *Tender Is the Night* Fitzgerald was keenly aware of Hemingway's achievement and found it necessary to make warning notes to himself: "Beware Ernest in this scene" and "Now a cheerful scene but remember to avoid Hemmingway"—referring to scenes that could have been handled in the clipped Hemingway dialogue.

The next meeting between Fitzgerald and Hemingway in January 1933 was spoiled because Fitzgerald was on a bender in New York. The occasion was a lunch with Edmund Wilson, at which Fitzgerald quarreled with both of them. Fitzgerald's *Notebook* includes his analysis of this reunion: "Very strong personalities must confine themselves in mutual conversation to very gentle subjects. Everything eventually transpires—but if they start at a very high pitch as at the last meeting of Ernest, Bunny and me, their meeting is spoiled. It does not matter who sets the theme or what it is." Fitzgerald dutifully reported to Perkins on 19 January:

> I was in New York for three days last week on a terrible bat. I was about to call you up when I completely collapsed and laid in bed for twenty-four hours groaning. [Fitzgerald had called Perkins.] Without a doubt the boy is getting too old for such tricks. Ernest told me he concealed from you the fact that I was in such rotten shape. . . . Am going on the water-wagon from the first of February to the first of April but don't tell Ernest because he has long convinced himself that I am an incurable alcoholic, due to the fact that we almost always meet on parties. I am *his* alcoholic just like Ring is mine and do not want to disillusion him, tho even Post stories must be done in a state of sobriety."

This 1933 meeting may have prompted Fitzgerald's *Notebook* entry: "I talk with the authority of failure—Ernest with the authority of success. We could never sit across the table again." Hemingway's reaction, expressed in January and February letters to Perkins, was that Scott could only be saved by two things: Zelda's death or a stomach ailment that would make it impossible for him to drink. Hemingway blamed Scott's "damned, bloody romanticism" and "cheap irish love of defeat." He'd like to see Scott sober. Fitzgerald remained more than loyal to Hemingway: he was pro-

Scott and Zelda Fitzgerald at the time of Tender Is the Night.

tective. When Gertrude Stein's *The Autobiography of Alice B. Toklas* appeared in 1933 with its belittling remarks about Hemingway, Fitzgerald was angry and phoned Perkins to find out if Ernest was upset.

From December 1933 to February 1934 Hemingway was on safari in Africa. *Tender Is the Night* was completed in the late fall of 1933, and it began appearing serially in *Scribner's Magazine* with the January 1934 issue. Perkins predicted to Hemingway on 7 February that Fitzgerald would be "completely reinstated" by *Tender Is the Night;* after revision it will be "a masterpiece of its kind." Writing to Perkins about the novel, Fitzgerald observed in March:

One time I had a talk with Ernest Hemingway, and I told him, against all the logic that was then current, that I was the tortoise and he was the hare, and that's the truth of the matter, that everything that I have ever attained has been through long and persistent struggle while it is Ernest who has a touch of genius which enables him to bring off extraordinary things with facility.

Tender Is the Night was published on 12 April 1934 in a first printing of 7600 copies; it required two more small printings and was dead after 15,000 copies. The novel did not recover the money Fitzgerald had borrowed from Scribners against it. The critical reception was disappointing, and it has become a cliché that the socially conscious critics of the thirties dismissed the novel because it dealt with wealthy American expatriates in the twenties. Study of the reviews does not support this interpretation. The reviewers were far more disturbed by the structure of the novel than by the material, finding the flashback plan confusing.

Although their friendship had cooled, Fitzgerald would come up fighting for Hemingway. One night in April 1934 James Thurber was with Fitzgerald in Tony's saloon on 52nd Street in New York when Fitzgerald overheard two men "not unlike the Killers in Hemingway's story" disparaging Hemingway. He stood up and said to them, "I am Scott Fitzgerald." Before he could demand an apology, the men walked away. Fitzgerald was reputedly sober at the time. In his account of that long drinking night, Thurber is alone in claiming that Fitzgerald held his liquor well.

Hemingway wrote to Perkins on 30 April complaining that *Tender Is the Night* was emotionally unsound. By using Gerald and Sara Murphy (to whom the novel was dedicated) as the models for Dick and Nicole Diver, Scott created unconvincing characters who behave in ways that the Murphys would never act. Scott has so "lousy much talent" that he almost brought it off; but he can't think straight. Scott never learned his trade, and he doesn't know anything. He hasn't truly imagined his characters because he doesn't know what people are like to begin with. The novel is false. Perkins replied on 3 May admitting that much of what Hemingway said about *Tender* is true, but noting that "a great deal of good writing has come from a sort of adolescent romanticism."

All of Scott's troubles are based on his inner confusion and unreal ideas about fundamentals. Perkins doesn't think Scott's hopelessness is justified, but it is useless to try to talk to him about it. In an undated letter Hemingway admitted to Perkins that *Tender* is much better than he had said in his letter; he was only analyzing the weakness of the novel and had not given credit to its merits. Perkins replied on 23 May that *Tender* has too much extraneous material Scott couldn't bear to cut. The basic illusion and conflict in Scott are responsible for the defects of *Tender,* although *Gatsby* was "fitted to the illusion and conflict."

While Hemingway and Perkins were corresponding about *Tender,* Fitzgerald was anxiously awaiting Hemingway's reaction. A month after publication Fitzgerald wrote from the apartment he had moved to from "La Paix." This is the first surviving letter between them since 1929.

1307 Park Avenue,
Baltimore, Maryland,
May 10, 1934.

Dear Ernest:

Did you like the book? For God's sake drop me a line and tell me one way or another. You can't hurt my feelings. I just want to get a few intelligent slants at it to get some of the reviewers jargon out of my head.

Ever Your Friend
Scott

All I meant about the editing [of *Winner Take Nothing*] was that if I'd been in Max's place I'd have urged you to hold the book for more material. It had neither the surprise of I.O.T (nessessessarily) nor its unity. And it did not have *as large a proportion* of 1st flight stories as M.W.W. I think in a "general presentation" way this could have been attoned for by sheer bulk. Take that opinion for what it's worth.

On the other hand: you can thank God you missed this publishing season! I am 5th best seller in the country + havn't broken 12,000.

Winner Take Nothing, Hemingway's third short-story collection, had been published in October 1933. Fitzgerald's previous comment on it has not been found. *Winner* was the least impressive of Hemingway's three story volumes, with only two major stories—"A Clean, Well-Lighted Place" and "The Gambler, the Nun, and the Radio." It included weak stories like "The Mother of a Queen," "One Reader Writes," "Homage to Switzerland," and "A Day's Wait." Even so, it had a first printing of 20,300 copies and outsold *Tender Is the Night*.

Hemingway sent Fitzgerald a harsh assessment of *Tender Is the Night* from Key West on 28 May 1934. Most of this three-page typed letter develops the criticism already made to Perkins that Scott distorted the Murphys into the Divers by combining them with the Fitzgeralds. Writers are supposed to invent truly. Although there are wonderful things in the novel, and although Scott can write better than anyone else, *Tender* is faked. Hemingway says that Scott could never think, but now he has stopped listening and has dried up as a writer. "We are like lousy damned acrobats but we make some might fine jumps, bo, and they have all these other acrobats that won't jump." He urges Scott to keep writing and stop thinking about masterpieces—again repeating the charge that Gilbert Seldes' review of *Gatsby* had blocked him. "Forget your personal tragedy. We are all bitched from the start. . . . But when you get the damned hurt use it—don't cheat with it. . . . About this time I wouldn't blame you if you gave me a burst. Jesus, it's marvellous to tell other pepole how to write, live, die etc. . . . You see, Bo, you're not a tragic character. Neither am I. All we are is writers and what we should do is write. Of all people on earth you needed discipline in your work and instead you marry someone who is jealous of your work, wants to compete with you and ruins you. It's not as simple as that and I thought Zelda was crazy the first time I met her and you complicated it even more by being in love with her and, of course you're a rummy. But you're no more of a rummy than Joyce is and most good writers are. . . . You are twice as good now as you were at the time you think you were so marvellous. . . . All you need to do is write truly and not care about what the fate of it is." On the envelope Hemingway added that he had not mentioned the parts of the novel he liked, but Scott knows which parts are good. He also acknowledges that Scott is right about *Winner Take Nothing.*

Though clearly hurt, Fitzgerald sent a calm six-page typed reply.

> 1307 Park Avenue,
> Baltimore, Maryland,
> June 1, 1934.

Dear Ernest:

Your letter crossed, or almost crossed, one of mine which I am glad now I didn't send, because the old charming frankness of your letter cleared up the foggy atmosphere through which I felt it was difficult for us to talk any more.

Because I'm going egoist on you in a moment, I want

to say that just exactly what you suggested, that the edition of that Chinamen-running story in the *Cosmopolitan*[39] would have given Winner Take Nothing the weight that it needed was in my head too. Allow me one more criticism, that while I admire your use of purely abstract titles I do not think that one was a particularly fortunate choice.

Next to go to the mat with you on a couple of technical points. The reason I had written you a letter was that Dos[40] dropped in in passing through and said you had brought up about my book what we talked about once in a cafe on the Avenue de Neuilly about composite characters. Now, I don't entirely dissent from the theory but I don't believe you can try to prove your point on such a case as Bunny using his own father as the sire of John Dos Passos, or in the case of this book that covers ground that you personally paced off about the same time I was doing it. In either of those cases how could you trust your own detachment? If you had never met any of the originals then your opinion would be more convincing.

Following this out a little farther, when does the proper and logical combination of events, cause and effect, etc. end and the field of imagination begin? Again you may be entirely right because I suppose you were applying the idea particularly to the handling of the creative faculty in one's mind rather than to the effect upon the stranger reading it. Nevertheless, I am not sold on the subject, and especially to account for the big flaws of *Tender* on that ground doesn't convince me. Think of the case of the Renaissance artists, and of the Elizabethan dramatists, the first having to superimpose a medieval conception of science and archeology, etc. upon the bible story; and in the second, of Shakespeare's trying to interpret the results of his own observation of the life around him on the basis of Plutarch's Lives and Hollinshed's Chronicles. There you must admit that the feat of building a monument out of three kinds of marble was brought off. You can accuse me justly of not having the power to bring it off, but a theory that it can't be done is

39 "One Trip Across."
40 John Dos Passos.

highly questionable. I make this point with such per-
sistence because such a conception, if you stick to it,
might limit your own choice of materials. The idea can
be reduced simply to: you can't say *accurately* that composite characterization hurt my book, but that it only
hurt it for you.

To take a case specifically, that of Gerald and Sara.
I don't know how much you think you know about my
relations with them over a long time, but from certain
remarks that you let drop, such as one "Gerald threw you
over," I guess that you didn't even know the beginning
of our relations. In that case you hit on the exact oppo-
site of the truth.

I think it is obvious that my respect for your artistic
life is absolutely unqualified, that save for a few of the
dead or dying old men you are the only man writing fiction in America that I look up to very much. There are
pieces and paragraphs of your work that I read over and
over—in fact, I stopped myself doing it for a year and a
half because I was afraid that your particular rhythms
were going to creep in on mine by process of infiltration.
Perhaps you will recognize some of your remarks in *Tender,* but I did every damn thing I could to avoid that.
(By the way, I didn't read the Wescott story of Villefranche sailors till I'd done my own version.[41] Think that
was the wisest course, for me anyhow, and got a pleasant
letter from him in regard to the matter.)

To go back to my theme song, the second technical
point that might be of interest to you concerns direct
steals from an idea of yours, an idea of Conrad's and a
few lines out of David-into-Fox-Garnett. The theory back
of it I got from Conrad's preface to *The Nigger,* that the
purpose of a work of fiction is to appeal to the lingering
after-effects in the reader's mind as differing from, say,
the purpose of oratory or philosophy which leave respec-
tively leave people in a fighting or thoughtful mood. The
second contribution to the burglary was your trying to
work out some such theory in your troubles with the very
end of *A Farewell to Arms.* I remember that your first
draft—or at least the first one I saw—gave a sort of old-

[41] "The Sailor," *Good-Bye Wisconsin* (1928).

fashioned Alger book summary of the future lives of the characters: "The priest became a priest under Fascism," etc., and you may remember my suggestion to take a burst of eloquence from anywhere in the book that you could find it and tag off with that; you were against this idea because you felt that the true line of a work of fiction was to take a reader up to a high emotional pitch but then let him down or ease him off. You gave no aesthetic reason for this—nevertheless, you convinced me. The third piece of burglary contributing to this symposing was my admiration of the dying fall in the aforesaid Garnett's book and I imitated it as accurately as it is humanly decent in my own ending of *Tender*, telling the reader in the last pages that, after all, this is just a casual event, and trying to let *him* come to bat for *me* rather than going out to shake his nerves, whoop him up, then leaving him rather in a condition of a frustrated woman in bed. (Did that ever happen to you in your days with MacCallagan or McKisco,[42] Sweetie?)

Thanks again for your letter which was damned nice, and my absolute best wishes to all of you (by the way, where did you ever get the idea that I didn't like Pauline, or that I didn't like her as much as I should? Of all that time of life the only temperamental coolness that I ever felt toward any of the people we ran around with was toward Ada MacLeish, and even in that case it was never any more than that. I have honestly never gone in for hating. My temporary bitternesses toward people have all been ended by what Freud called an inferiority complex and Christ called "Let him without sin—" I remember the day he said it. We were justlikethat then; we tossed up for who was going to go through with it—and he lost.

I am now asking only $5,000 for letters. Make out the check to Malcolm Republic, c/o *The New Cowlick*.[43]

Ever your friend,

Scott

P.S. Did you ever see my piece about Ring in the *New Cowlick*—I think you'd have liked it.

---

42 "MacCallagan" is a composite name for McAlmon and Callaghan. Albert McKisco's name in *Tender Is the Night* was a play on "McAlmon."
43 Malcolm Cowley was an editor of *The New Republic*.

P.S.S. This letter and questions require no answers. You are "write" that I no longer listen, but my case histories seem to go in largely for the same magazines, and with simple people I get polite. But I listen to you and would like damn well to hear your voice again.

This letter opens up the question of possible cross-pollinization between Fitzgerald and Hemingway. The places in their work that may indicate such an influence are rare—for example, the series of "Yes" answers by Anson Hunter in "The Rich Boy," when he visits Paula and her husband, resembles Hemingway's dialogue. The evidence is slender. Fitzgerald and Hemingway had developed their styles before they met in 1925; they were beyond imitation. Nevertheless, other forms of influence were possible, both personal and aesthetic. Fitzgerald probably drew on Hemingway for Tommy Barban, the soldier of fortune in *Tender Is the Night*. The specific aesthetic influence of Hemingway on *Tender* that Fitzgerald acknowledges in his letter was the theory about the function of the ending of a novel. When they discussed *A Farewell to Arms* in 1929, Hemingway had persuaded Fitzgerald that a novel should not end on an emotional peak—a principle Fitzgerald found substantiated in the work of Joseph Conrad and David Garnett. The formulation of the "dying fall" ending was collaborative, resulting from discussions between Fitzgerald and Hemingway. Soon after *Tender* was published, Fitzgerald commented to H. L. Mencken about the reviewers' failure to understand the intention of the novel: ". . . the motif of the 'dying fall' was absolutely deliberate and did not come from any diminuition of vitality, but from a definite plan. That particular trick is one that Ernest Hemmingway and I worked out—probably from Conrad's preface to 'The Nigger'—and it has been the greatest 'credo' in my life, ever since I decided that I would rather be an artist than a careerist." In 1936 Fitzgerald explained to John O'Hara:

—the only effect I ever had on Ernest was to get him in a receptive mood and say let's cut everything that goes before this. The pieces got mislaid and he caould never find the part that I said to cut out. And so he published it without that and later we agreed that it was a very wise cut. This is not literally true and I don't want it established as part of the Hemingway Legend, but it's just about as far as one writer can go in helping another. Years later when Ernest was writing *Farewell to Arms* he was in doubt about the ending and marketed around to half a dozen people for their advice. I worked like hell on the idea and only succeeded in evolving a philosophy in his mind utterly contrary to everything that he thought an ending should be and later convinced me that he was right and made me end *Tender Is the Night* on a fade away instead of a staccato.

When Edmund Wilson was editing *The Crack-Up*, he showed Fitzgerald's carbon copy of this letter to Hemingway, who annotated it: "This is all nonsense. EH He is referring to my cutting the first paragraphs of a story called Fifty grand. It is a funny story which I would be glad to give you if you like EH."

A year after publication of *Tender* Fitzgerald admitted to Perkins that Part III of his novel was not tightly organized: "If I had one more crack at it cold sober I believe it might have made a great difference. Even Ernest commented on sections that were needlessly included and as an artist he is as near as I know for a final reference."

In 1933 Arnold Gingrich, editor of the new magazine *Esquire*, made a deal with Hemingway to pay him *Esquire*'s top price of $250 for a series of monthly articles called letters. A passionate admirer of both Hemingway's and Fitzgerald's writing, Gingrich was happy to add Fitzgerald to his roster of authors at $250 per contribution the next year. Fitzgerald's first *Esquire* appearance was "Show Mr. and Mrs. F. to Number—," a two-part article by-lined as by Scott and Zelda Fitzgerald in the May and June 1934 issues.

During the summer of 1934 Perkins was trying to expedite publication of Fitzgerald's fourth story collection, *Taps at Reveille*, which Fitzgerald was holding in order to remove the story passages that he had incorporated in *Tender*. Perkins assured him that such repetition is permissible. "Hem has done it." Fitzgerald replied rather stiffly on 24 August: "The fact that Ernest has let himself repeat here and there a phrase would be no possible justification for me doing the same. Each of us has his virtues and one of mine happens to be a great sense of exactitude about my work. He might be able to afford a lapse in that line where I wouldn't be and after all I have got to be the final judge of what is appropriate in these cases." *Taps* was published on 20 March 1935 in a printing of 5000 copies—which satisfied the demand. The stories were largely retrospective, with seven of the Basil and Josephine stories; the collection also included three of Fitzgerald's best stories—"Crazy Sunday," "The Last of the Belles," and "Babylon Revisited."

After *Tender Is the Night* Fitzgerald projected a novel set in ninth-century France, an account of the attempts by young Philippe, Count of Villefranche, to reclaim his father's territory. The characterization of Philippe was based on Ernest Hemingway. Fitzgerald made this *Notebook* entry: "Just as Stendahl's portrait of a Byronic man made *Le Rouge et Noir* so couldn't *my* portrait of Ernest as Phillipe make the real modern man." It was clear that *Tender* was not going to solve Fitzgerald's money problems, and his ability to write stories for *The Saturday Evening Post* was fading. His plan was to treat the Philippe material as a series of stories in *Redbook* for ready cash and then to revise the stories into a novel. The first story, "In the Darkest Hour," published in October 1934, may have been written as early as April. Three more Philippe stories were written, which *Redbook* bought with increasing reluctance; and Fitzgerald abandoned the project in 1935—at least for the time being. While he was working on them, Fitzgerald had a scare when he learned that Hemingway had a new book ready. On 20 November 1934 Fitzgerald wrote to Perkins: "I hope to God it isn't the crusading story that he once had in mind, for I would hate like hell for my 9th century novel to have to compete with *that*." Hemingway's new book was *Green Hills of Africa*.

The medieval stories—Fitzgerald's only extended attempt at historical fiction—were bad and have been largely ignored. Fitzgerald later wrote Perkins: "You will remember that the plan in the beginning was tremendously ambitious—there was to have been Philippe as a young man founding his fortunes—Philippe as a middle-aged man participating in the Captian founding of France as a nation—Philippe as an old man and the consolidation of the feudal system. It was to have covered a span of about sixty years from 880 A.D. to 950." In the first four stories twenty-year-old Philippe enters the Loire Valley, organizes the peasants, defeats a band of marauding Vikings, builds a stronghold, treats with the powers of Church and State, and enters into a compact with a witchcraft cult. He is determined, resourceful, and unbelievable. The most obvious difficulty was linguistic, as Fitzgerald tried to convey the speech of medieval French peasants by making them talk like American sharecroppers. Philippe uses a kind of hardboiled slang that seems to derive from the pulp detective magazines. The effect is incongruous and even inadvertently funny: " 'Call me "Sire!" .... And remember; There's no bedroom talk floating around this precinct!' " Anyone who did not know that Philippe was modeled on Hemingway would not be likely to make the identification. There is nothing to indicate that Hemingway recognized himself—if he ever read the stories. Fitzgerald never really gave up on the medieval material; and in 1939 when he was planning *The Last Tycoon* he was still considering whether it would be better to return to Philippe instead.

In May 1934, after his return from Africa, Hemingway acquired the *Pilar,* a 38-foot Wheeler cruiser, and began inviting friends to Key West for fishing trips. Arnold Gingrich, the editor of *Esquire,* was invited for December and proposed bringing Fitzgerald along. Hemingway agreed, but on 3 December Fitzgerald wired:

> DEAR ERNEST SEEMS IMPOSSIBLE TO GET DOWN THIS WEEK AND I CERTAINLY REGRET IT AND I APPRECIATE YOUR INVITATION HAD SO MANY THINGS TO TALK TO YOU ABOUT WITH BEST WISHES ALWAYS TO YOU AND YOURS = SCOTT.

Gingrich and Fitzgerald cooked up the excuse that his mother's illness prevented him from leaving Baltimore; but the real reason was that Fitzgerald was intimidated by the prospect of being with Hemingway in his Florida principality. He explained to Perkins, "Your suggestion to go to Key West is tempting as hell but I don't know whether it would be advisable on either Ernest's account or mine." Perkins was scheduled to go to Key West in January 1935 to read the typescript of *Green Hills of Africa.* He, too, asked permission to bring Fitzgerald. Hemingway replied on 28 December 1934 that he would like to see Scott after the revision of *Green Hills,* but that it would be hard to work with Scott there because he would try to help. Scott's advice about revising a book is worth-

Hemingway at Key West.

less. Ernest will show Max Scott's suggestion for improving *A Farewell to Arms* by inserting a scene in which Frederic Henry reads about the American Marines while Catherine is in labor.

On 27 February 1935 Perkins reported to Hemingway that Fitzgerald was on the wagon, and suggested that Hemingway might be able to encourage him. Through March–June Perkins sent Hemingway bulletins announcing that Fitzgerald was still on the wagon. Whether he did quit drinking altogether is questionable. Like most alcoholics, he defined being on the wagon in special ways; at this time it meant drinking only beer. In 1935 Fitzgerald became anxious about a recurrence of tuberculosis and began making trips to the mountain area around Asheville, North Carolina. After Zelda suffered her third breakdown, Fitzgerald placed her in the Highland Hospital at Asheville in April 1936 and moved to the Grove Park Inn. The 1935–1937 period has become known as "The Crack-Up," from the essay Fitzgerald wrote about it. No longer able to produce the short stories that had brought $4000 each from *The Saturday Evening Post,* he sank into debt, despair, and illness. His income came from an occasional sale to the slick magazines (which had cut his price), $250 checks from *Esquire* (which would take virtually anything he submitted), and advances from Harold Ober (which were really loans).

Hemingway's judgment of his work continued to matter to Scott. When Perkins relayed a message from Hemingway on 8 April 1935—"A strange thing is that in retrospect his Tender is the Night gets better and better. I wish you would tell him I said so"—Fitzgerald pasted it in his scrapbook. He responded to Perkins—not to Hemingway. "Thanks for the message from Ernest. I'd like to see him too and I always think of my friendship with him as being one of the high spots in my life. But I still believe that such things have a mortality, perhaps in reaction to their very excessive life, and that we will never again see very much of each other. I appreciate what he said about 'Tender is the Night.' "

On 13 May 1935 Fitzgerald tried to arrange a reunion with Hemingway, promising that he would be sober:

WANT TO SEE YOU AS AM GOING TO CAROLINA FOR SUMMER COULD MAKE THREE DAY STAY KEYWEST ARRIVING THIS THURSDAY BUT WANT [sic] TO INTERFERE YOUR PLANS STOP NOT UP TO ANYTHING STRENUOUS PROBABLY RESULT OF TEATOTALING SINCE JANUARY WIRE THIRTEEN NAUGHT SEVEN PARK AVENUE BALTIMORE = SCOTT.

Pauline wired that Ernest was in Bimini.

Green Hills of Africa, Hemingway's nonfiction novel about his safari, was published 25 October 1935 after serialization in *Scribner's Magazine.* The first printing of 10,550 copies satisfied the demand for the book. The reviews were mixed, with several critics objecting to the irrelevance of the material to contemporary problems. Bernard De Voto in *The Saturday Review of Literature* called it "a pretty small book for a big man to write." In the *New Masses* Granville Hicks urged Hemingway to write a novel about a strike. Hemingway anticipated the response from the Left and had eloquently answered it in the book: "A country, finally, erodes and the dust blows away, the people all die and none of them were of any importance permanently, except those who practised the arts, and these now wish to cease their work because it is too lonely, too hard to do, and is not fashionable. A thousand years makes economics silly and a work of art endures for ever, but it is very difficult to do and now it is not fashionable." *Green Hills of Africa* includes an oblique reference to Fitzgerald. Discoursing on the ways American writers are destroyed, Hemingway says that at present there are "two good writers who cannot write because they have lost confidence through reading critics. If they wrote, sometimes it would be good and sometimes not so good and sometimes it would be quite bad, but the good would get out. But they have read the critics and they must write masterpieces. The masterpieces the critics said they wrote. They weren't masterpieces, of course. They were just quite good books. So now they cannot write at all. The critics have made them impotent." Those writers are not identified, but one is clearly Fitzgerald. Here again Hemingway advances his pet theory that Fitzgerald was blocked by Gilbert Seldes' review of *The Great Gatsby*. Fitzgerald's reaction to this passage is unknown, but he certainly read it. He read everything Hemingway wrote.

Fitzgerald's letter to Hemingway about *Green Hills of Africa* is lost, but it obviously expressed reservations. Hemingway responded from Key West on 16 December saying that he is happy to see that Scott still doesn't know what is a good book. Ernest recently found Scott's letter of advice about *A Farewell to Arms,* and the letter about *Green Hills* is more of the same. Scott is like a brilliant mathematician who always gets the wrong answers. Despite Scott's bad drinking behavior, his friends are still fond of him, Sara Murphy talked to Ernest for an afternoon about Scott. Ernest started for Asheville to see Scott last September, but had to change his plans. He wants to talk to Scott. "The more I think back to it the better book Tender Is The Night is." He invites Scott to Key West and suggests that they go to Havana for the Joe Louis fight (which was canceled).

On the 21st of December 1935 Hemingway replied to a gloomy letter from Fitzgerald—which has not been found. He invites Scott to Key West and lectures him on his regret for his lost youth. "If you really feel blue enough get yourself heavily insured and I'll see you can get killed [in Cuba] . . . and I'll write you a fine obituary . . . and we can take your liver out and give it to the Princeton Museum, your heart to the Plaza Hotel, one lung to Max Perkins and the other to George Horace Lorimer. If we can still find your balls I will take them via the Ile de France to Paris and down to Antibes and have them cast into the sea off Eden Roc and we will get MacLeish to write a Mystic Poem to be read at that Catholic School (Newman?) you went to. Would you like me to write the mystic poem now. Let' see." An eighteen-line free-verse parody followed.

By August 1936 eleven Fitzgerald pieces had appeared in *Esquire,* most of which were retrospective essays. The contributions that attracted the most attention were a group of confessional articles—beginning with "The Crack-Up" in the February 1936 issue—in which Fitzgerald analyzed his "emotional bankruptcy." In "Pasting It Together" (March 1936) Fitzgerald stipulated his admiration for Hemingway: "That a third contemporary had been an artistic conscience for me—I had not imitated his infectious style, because my own style, such as it is, was formed before he published anything, but there was an awful pull toward him when I was in a spot." Hemingway was not named, but the identification was obvious.

Perkins and Ober felt that these articles were seriously damaging Fitzgerald's reputation and urged him to stop writing them. Ernest felt more strongly about them, regarding such public confessions as shameless and contemptible. Hemingway wrote to John Dos Passos expressing shock at "The Crack-Up" when he read it in January. On 7 February Hemingway wrote to Perkins about Fitzgerald's perverse pride in defeat as revealed in the "miserable" *Esquire* articles. Scott could never think straight, but he has a marvelous talent which he is wasting by publicly whining. If Scott had been in the war he would have been shot for cowardice. Ernest admits that it is rotten to attack Scott after all his troubles, but his troubles were his own fault. The only thing that would help Scott is work for its own sake—not for money. Scott has passed from youth to senility but avoided manhood. Ernest wishes he could help him.

Hemingway maintained his friendship with Gerald and Sara Murphy during the thirties. His letters to the Murphys mention Fitzgerald infrequently and contemptuously. After publication of "The Crack-Up," Hemingway compared the troubles the Murphys have experienced to Napoleon's retreat from Moscow—from which Scott would have deserted during the first week. Describing how amberjacks chased a fish he had hooked, Hemingway comments that they chased the fish because it ran: "Make a note of that for Mr. FitzGerald."

It is possible that Hemingway's reaction to "The Crack-Up" articles was intensified by seeing them in the magazine where he was the star contributor. But *Esquire* was Fitzgerald's only dependable market. The August 1936 issue included Fitzgerald's "After-

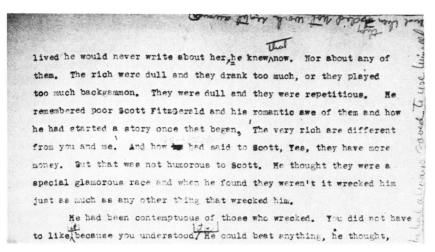

University of Texas Library.

noon of an Author" and Hemingway's "The Snows of Kilimanjaro." "Afternoon of an Author" is a confessional sketch about a writer who is unable to write. "The Snows of Kilimanjaro," a long story about a dying writer who has become corrupted by his marriage to a wealthy woman, includes the comment that "poor Scott Fitzgerald" was "wrecked" by his "romantic awe" of the rich. Fitzgerald's 16 July 1936 response from Asheville was remarkably controlled:

Dear Ernest:

Please lay off me in print. If I choose to write *de profundis* sometimes it doesn't mean I want friends praying aloud over my corpse. No doubt you meant it kindly but it cost me a night's sleep. And when you incorporate it (the story) in a book would you mind cutting my name?

It's a fine story—one of your best—even though the "Poor Scott Fitzgerald ect" rather spoiled it for me

Ever Your Friend

Scott

Riches have *never* facinated me, unless combined with the greatest charm or distinction.

Perkins had been present when Mary Colum delivered the rejoinder to Hemingway: "The only difference between the rich and other people is that the rich have more money." Perkins did not mention the "poor Scott" reference in his 21 July letter to Hemingway praising "Snows." Perkins was satisfied to write his cousin Elizabeth Lemmon, who was Fitzgerald's friend, on 16 August calling Hemingway's reference to Fitzgerald "contemptible" and telling her about the Hemingway-Colum exchange.

Hemingway wrote to Perkins on the 22nd of July commenting on Fitzgerald's letter of protest, which he found strange coming from a man who had published the "Crack-Up" articles. Hemingway reports he told Scott that for five years he has refrained from writing about people he knows—because he was sorry for them—but now Ernest is going to stop being a gentleman and return to being a novelist. Hemingway's letter to Fitzgerald does not survive; Arnold Gingrich read it and has described it in "Scott, Ernest and Whoever" (1966) as "brutal," with language "that you'd hesitate to use on a yellow dog." Why did Gingrich print "the poor Scott" passage in *Esquire?* Although Gingrich never answered this question, the explanation seems clear enough. Gingrich was so proud to have Hemingway as a regular contributor in *Esquire* that he did not want to run the risk of alienating him. Gingrich's 1966 article reports that when he was fishing with Hemingway at Bimini in June 1936 he committed the blunder of praising Fitzgerald's style and was shushed by a member of Hemingway's Bimini entourage: " 'We don't say things like that around here.' " Gingrich was himself obeying the don't-upset-Ernest rule: "Thinking back on it now, it occurs to me that at that very moment the presses were turning, back in Chicago, with the August '36 issue of Esquire containing the first printed appearance of *The Snows of Kilimanjaro* with its line, later changed, referring to 'poor Scott Fitzgerald,' but I'm sure I never gave that a thought at the time."

On the 15th of September—two months after "Snows" appeared—Fitzgerald wrote to Beatrice Dance, with whom he had engaged in a brief affair in North Carolina, providing a report of his correspondence with Hemingway:

> As to Ernest, at first I resented his use of my name in the story and I wrote him a somewhat indignant letter, telling him it must not be republished in a book. He answered, agreeing, but rather resentfully and saying that he felt that since I had chosen to expose my private life so "shamelessly" in *Esquire,* he felt that it was sort of an open season for me, and I wrote him a hell of a letter which would have been sudden death for somebody the next time we met, and decided, hell let it go. Too often literary men allow themselves to get into inter-necine quarrels and finish about as victoriously as most of the nations at the end of the World War. I consider it an example of approaching maturity on my part and am proud of my self control. He is quite as nervously broken down as I am but it manifests itself in different ways. His inclination is toward megalomania and mine toward melancholy.

Four days later Fitzgerald wrote to Perkins:

> I feel that I must tell you something which at first seemed better to leave alone: I wrote Ernest about that

story of his, asking him in the most measured terms not to use my name in future pieces of fiction. He wrote me back a crazy letter, telling me about what a great Writer he was and how much he loved his children, but yielding the point—"If I should out live him—" which he doubted. To have answered it would have been like fooling with a lit firecracker. Somehow I love that man, no matter what he says or does, but just one more crack and I think I would have to throw my weight with the gang and lay him. No one could ever hurt him in his first books but he has completely lost his head and the duller he gets about it, the more he is like a punch-drunk pug fighting himself in the movies.

Carlos Baker, Hemingway's biographer, suggests that "Snows" reveals his morbid concern that he might die without having fulfilled his talent. He had not, in fact, published a novel in seven years. Fitzgerald recognized that around 1936 Hemingway underwent a personality shift—as though he had come to believe the Hemingway legends. Nonetheless, Fitzgerald was determined to avoid a final break with the living writer he most admired.

Perkins replied to Fitzgerald: "As for what Ernest did, I resented it, and when it comes to book publication, I shall have it out with him. It is odd about it too because I was present when that reference was made to the rich, and the retort given, and you were many miles away." Perkins did not, however, tell Fitzgerald about the actual exchange between Hemingway and Mary Colum.

On 19 March 1937 Perkins assured Fitzgerald that "poor Scott" would be deleted from "Snows." "As for Ernest, I know he will cut that piece out of his story. He spoke to me a while ago about it, and his feelings toward you are far different from what you seem to suspect. I think he had some queer notion that he would give you a 'jolt' and that it might be good for you, or something like that. Anyhow, he means to take it out."

Given the hurt generated by "The Snows of Kilimanjaro," it is revealing that Fitzgerald turned to Hemingway for help in September 1936 when he was again publicly humiliated. On his fortieth birthday—24 September 1936—Fitzgerald gave an interview in Asheville to Michel Mok, which appeared in the *New York Post*

the next day headlined: "The Other Side of Paradise/Scott Fitzgerald, 40,/Engulfed in Despair/Broken in Health He Spends
Birthday Re-/gretting That He Has Lost Faith in His Star." The
article portrayed him as a broken, crying drunk. When he saw it
Fitzgerald attempted suicide by swallowing morphine, which he
vomited up. Fitzgerald felt that Mok had ruined him, the more so
since the interview was picked up in *Time*. Among the Fitzgerald
Papers there is a Western Union form dated 28 September for a
wire to Hemingway at Cook City, Montana, written in an uniden-
tified hand: "If you ever wanted to help me your chance is now Stop
A man named Michael Moch has taken advantage of an interview
to spread me all over the N.Y. Evening Post in an absurd position
Stop It cuts in on me directly and indirectly—Scott." There is no
evidence that this wire was sent, but Fitzgerald sent another wire
to Hemingway c/o Scribners, which was probably forwarded. Hemingway replied that he had not seen the Mok article but was ready
to help. Fitzgerald wired back:

WIRED UNDER IMPRESSION YOU WERE IN NEW YORK NOTHING
CAN BE DONE AT LONG RANGE AND ON COOLER CONSIDERA-
TION SEEMS NOTHING TO BE DONE ANYHOW THANKS BEST
ALWAYS SCOTT.

On the first of October 1936 Perkins sent Hemingway a situation report on Fitzgerald. "I don't know what you could do for
him, but the interview he gave the Post was frightful. It seemed as
if Scott were bent on destroying himself." Scott had trusted Mok
and said things that were not for publication, but the reporter
had betrayed Scott's confidence. Scott's mother left him $20,000,
and Perkins has told him that he must write for two years with this
inheritance. "I told him that this was the only way to answer what
this reporter had done." Perhaps, Perkins tells Hemingway, having
hit bottom, Scott may rebound from the shock of the *Post* article.
Perkins manages to find some comfort in the notion that "hardly
anybody reads the New York Post."

The Spanish Civil War broke out in July 1936, but Hemingway did not go to report it until March 1937. He was committed to
the Loyalists, who were backed by Russia, and for a time it ap-

peared that Hemingway had entered a period of political activism. The Left hoped so and began to welcome him into the fold, interpreting his involvement with the Loyalists as evidence that he had outgrown his egotistical and irrelevant interests. The Leftists were naive, for Hemingway's anti-Fascism never made him a pro-Communist. He was always suspicious of organizations and movements, trusting only his own instincts. Above all, Hemingway was suspicious of any attempt to organize writers, believing always that the writer must be a loner.

The hurt over "Snows" remained, but Fitzgerald maintained his interest in Hemingway's career and wrote Perkins predicting that the Spanish War would provide Hemingway with new material:

> Ernest ought to write a swell book now about Spain—real Richard Harding Davis reporting or better. (I mean not the sad jocosity of P.O.M.[44] passages or the mere callender of slaughter.) And speaking of Ernest, did I tell you that when I wrote asking him to cut me out of his story he answered, with ill grace, that he would—in fact he answered with such unpleasantness that it is hard to think he has any friendly feeling to me any more. Anyhow please remember that he agreed to do this if the story should come in with me still in it.

In Spain Hemingway began his liaison with writer Martha Gellhorn, who became his third wife in 1940. At the time of their meeting he was thirty-seven; she was twenty-nine. In the spring of 1937 Hemingway wrote war dispatches for the North American Newspaper Alliance and worked on a propaganda movie, *The Spanish Earth*.

On 4 June 1937 Hemingway addressed the American Writers' Congress at Carnegie Hall in New York. The meeting was sponsored by the League of American Writers, whose president was Donald Ogden Stewart—"Bill Gorton" in *The Sun Also Rises*, now a screenwriter and political activist. Earl Browder, the Secretary of the American Communist Party, was also on the program. Archibald MacLeish chaired the meeting. Hemingway's short speech was an attack on Fascism: "There is only one form of govern-

[44] In *Green Hills of Africa* Pauline was called P.O.M.(Poor old Mahmma).

ment that cannot produce good writers, and that system is fascism. For fascism is a lie told by bullies." Although the speech was not eloquent, it received thunderous applause from the audience, who regarded it as a symbolic event. Hemingway was with them. The most famous living American writer had joined the cause.

The Carnegie Hall meeting provided the occasion for the penultimate meeting between Fitzgerald and Hemingway. At this time Fitzgerald was coming out of his "Crack-Up" and was seeking movie employment as the only way to pay off his debts—which may have amounted to $40,000. Hemingway's appearance in New York was well-publicized in advance, and Fitzgerald probably made a trip from North Carolina to see him. The only evidence of this reunion is Fitzgerald's note mailed to Hemingway from the train at Washington on 5 June:

> It was fine to see you so well + full of life, Ernest. I hope you'll make your book fat—I know some of that *Esquire* work is too good to leave out. All best wishes to your Spanish trip—I wish we could meet more often. I don't feel I know you at all.
>
> Ever yours
Scott
>
> Going South always seems to me rather desolate + fatal and uneasy. This is no exception. Going north is a safe dull feeling.

The meeting appears to have been sober and friendly. It is noteworthy that even at this stage Fitzgerald retained an almost proprietary interest in Hemingway's career. Hemingway was considering including stories with *To Have and Have Not,* and Fitzgerald approved of the plan. (The published volume included only the novel.)

Harold Ober arranged a six-month contract for Fitzgerald at Metro-Goldwyn-Mayer for $1000 a week, with a renewal option for a year at $1250. Fitzgerald arrived in Hollywood the first week of July 1937. A few days later Hemingway came to show *The Spanish Earth* and raise money for the Loyalists. This occasion was the final meeting between F. Scott Fitzgerald and Ernest Hemingway. Lillian Hellman has published her recollections of this evening

Fitzgerald in Hollywood. Photo by Belle O'Hara.

(although she mis-dates it as occurring in 1938.) Fitzgerald was present when Hemingway showed *The Spanish Earth* at the home of Fredric March. Afterward some of the guests were invited to Dorothy Parker's house for drinks. Fitzgerald offered to drive Miss Hellman, but said he didn't want to go in. On the wagon and nervous, he was intimidated by Ernest. She coaxed Fitzgerald into the house. As they entered the living room, Hemingway—who had his back to the door—threw a glass into the fireplace. Fitzgerald wanted to leave but she took him to the kitchen, where Dashiell

Hammett was talking to Dorothy Parker. Miss Hellman does not recall if Fitzgerald talked to Hemingway and did not notice when Fitzgerald left. Some time later when Hemingway challenged Hammett to a spoon-bending contest in the Stork Club, Hammett said, "Why don't you go back to bullying Fitzgerald? Too bad he doesn't know how good he is. The best."

The morning after the movie showing, Fitzgerald wired Hemingway: THE PICTURE WAS BEYOND PRAISE AND SO WAS YOUR ATTITUDE = SCOTT. On 15 July Fitzgerald reported to Perkins: "I felt he was in a state of nervous tensity, that there was something almost religious about it."

At MGM Fitzgerald was put to work revising *A Yank at Oxford* and then was given the choice assignment to write the screenplay for Erich Maria Remarque's *Three Comrades*. He stayed on the wagon for the time being. Although he quarreled with producer Joseph Mankiewicz on *Three Comrades,* the movie was highly successful, and his option was picked up at the end of 1937. Fitzgerald's chief problem in Hollywood was that he could not work well with collaborators, which was the way most screenplays were put together. Shortly after his arrival he met Sheilah Graham, the English Hollywood columnist, who became his companion and lover. They made a life together, and Fitzgerald found a measure of happiness and even peace in Hollywood. Zelda Fitzgerald remained at Highland Hospital; Fitzgerald's visits to see her in North Carolina usually triggered his drinking bouts.

With Fitzgerald in Hollywood and Hemingway in Spain or Cuba or Sun Valley with Martha Gellhorn, Perkins continued to keep them informed about each other. In August 1937 Hemingway and critic Max Eastman engaged in a well-publicized brawl in Perkins' office. Eastman had referred to Hemingway's false hair-on-the-chest manner in reviewing *Death in the Afternoon,* which Hemingway interpreted as imputing that he was impotent. On 3 September Fitzgerald responded to Perkins' detailed account.

I was thoroughly amused by your descriptions, but what transpires is that Ernest did exactly the asinine thing that I knew he had it in him to do when he was out here. The fact that he lost his temper only for a minute does not mini-

[138]

mize the fact that he picked the exact wrong minute to do it. His discretion must have been at low ebb or he would not have again trusted the reporters at the boat.

He is living at the present in a world so entirely his own that it is impossible to help him, even if I felt close to him at the moment, which I don't. I like him so much, though, that I wince when anything happens to him, and I feel rather personally ashamed that it has been possible for imbeciles to dig at him and hurt him. After all, you would think that a man who has arrived at the position of being practically his country's most imminent writer, could be spared that yelping.

Hemingway's third novel, *To Have and Have Not,* was published on 15 October 1937. It was a disappointing work for his first novel in eight years, but it sold 36,000 copies—largely on the strength of Hemingway's reputation. *To Have and Have Not* did not represent eight years of work, and it wasn't really a novel. Occupied with Spain and Martha, he assembled a book from two previously published stories ("One Trip Across," *Cosmopolitan* [April 1934] and "The Tradesman's Return," *Esquire* [February 1936]), adding a long third section. It looked patched-together. The opening section was written in the first person and the other sections in the third person.

On 3 February 1938 Perkins reported to Hemingway that Fitzgerald had been in New York and was in good shape. Scott said that Ernest is "the most dynamic personality" in the world. Hemingway replied that he would have liked to see old Scott, but states that he never wanted to be dynamic; he just wanted to be a writer.

Fitzgerald continued to worry about "The Snows of Kilimanjaro," and on 4 March 1938 he reminded Perkins to remove his name when the story was published in book form:

> The enclosed letter . . . . shows quite definitely how a whole lot of people interpreted Ernest's crack at me in "Snows of K." When I called him on it, he promised in a letter that he would not reprint it in book form. Of course, since then, it has been in O'Brien's collection [*The Best Short Stories of 1937*], but I gather he can't help that. If, however, you are publishing a collection of his this fall, do keep in mind that he has

promised to make an elision of my name. It was a damned rotten thing to do, and with anybody but Ernest my tendency would be to crack back. Why did he think it would add to the strength of his story if I had become such a negligible figure? This is quite indefensible on any grounds.

Perkins reassured Fitzgerald on 9 March: "You know our position about Ernest's story "The Snows".—Don't be concerned about it." During the summer of 1938 Perkins was working with Hemingway on his collected short stories, *The First Forty-Nine Stories.* On the 9th of August Perkins reminded him about his promise to emend "Snows": "And by the way, you were going to take out F.S.F. weren't you, from 'The Snows of Kilimanjaro'?" Hemingway revised the passage but retained the name "Scott." Perkins responded on 23 August in his best diplomatic style:

> As to the Scott passage, you amended it very neatly.— But I greatly wish his name could come out altogether. If people reading the story do not identify "Scott" as F.S.F., it might as well be some other name (one realizes he is a writer in the very next sentence) and if they do identify him, it seems to me it takes them out of the story for a moment. It takes their attention to the question of what this means about Scott. You did take out the things that could hurt and I showed the amended passage to two people who had never read the story and they thought Scott might still feel badly, being very sensitive, but that they hardly thought there was much reason for it now. If his name could come out without hurting, it would be good.—But I'll bring up the matter when you are here.

After Hemingway came to New York, Perkins wrote to Fitzgerald on 1 September saying that he wishes he could talk to him about Ernest. Perkins is uncertain about Ernest's plan for a new work and would like to have Scott's reaction. Scribners is going to publish Ernest's collected stories. "One of the new stories is 'The Snows of Kilimanjaro' and you are not in it."

The final decision was to change "poor Scott Fitzgerald" to "poor Julian," leaving the rest of the passage unrevised. All subsequent Scribners printings have retained "Julian." Writing to Arthur Mizener in 1951 to acknowledge receipt of his biography of Fitzgerald, Hemingway remarked that Fitzgerald should have known that in "Snows" Harry would have mentioned Scott the same way that Fitzgerald used real things in his own writing. A. E. Hotchner has reported that in 1955 Hemingway told him it was time to put Scott back in the story.

The Fifth Column and The First Forty-Nine Stories was published 14 October 1938. *The Fifth Column,* Hemingway's first and only play, was a propagandistic treatment of the Scarlet Pimpernel-in-Madrid, but its topicality—and the fact that it was by Hemingway—attracted enough attention to secure a Broadway production of eighty-seven performances.

Fitzgerald tried to supervise his daughter's reading at Vassar by mail from Hollywood, and Hemingway was one of the authors he assigned her. On 15 November 1938 he reprimanded Scottie: "How you could possibly have missed the answer to my first question I don't know, unless you skipped pages 160 to 170 in *Farewell to Arms.*[45] Try again!"

When Thomas Wolfe's *The Web and the Rock* (1939) portrayed Perkins unflatteringly as Foxhall Edwards, Fitzgerald wrote to sympathize with Perkins on 25 February 1939: "It is astonishing what people will do though. Ernest's sharp turn against me always seemed to have pointless childish quality—so much so that I really never felt any resentment about it."

There is a published report of a final Hollywood reunion between Fitzgerald and Hemingway; *but it did not happen.* Aaron Latham's *Crazy Sundays* (1971) includes Charles Marquis Warren's account of how Hemingway came to board with Fitzgerald and Sheilah Graham at Malibu Beach in the summer of 1938. According to Warren—who was also living in the Malibu cottage—Hemingway was broke and Fitzgerald gave him a $25-a-week allowance. Warren reports that Hemingway worked on *For Whom the Bell Tolls* on the beach at night by lantern light, and he claims that Hemingway gave him one of the sleeping-bag scenes to read. One day, according to Warren, Fitzgerald took Hemingway to

[45] Chapters 23–24 in the first edition, Frederic Henry's parting from Catherine in Milan.

MGM. After calling producer Bernard Hyman a "Heeb," Hemingway insulted Louis B. Mayer, who had him thrown off the lot. *It did not happen. None of it ever happened.* Warren's account is not substantiated by anyone else, and Sheilah Graham—who was living with Fitzgerald—denies it. In the summer of 1938 Hemingway was in Key West and Wyoming; he did not start *For Whom the Bell Tolls* until 1939 in Cuba.

After Fitzgerald's MGM contract elapsed in January 1939, he free-lanced at other studios while planning a Hollywood novel. On 25 March 1939 Hemingway wrote Perkins that he had just re-read *Tender Is the Night* and was amazed by "how <u>excellent</u> much of it is." It would have been a fine novel if Scott could have integrated it better. Ernest wishes Scott could have kept writing. Is Scott all finished? Ernest asks Perkins to give Scott his great affection, admitting, "(I always had a very stupid little boy feeling of superiority about Scott—like a tough durable little boy sneering at a delicate but talented little boy.) Reading that novel much of it was so good it was frightening." Fitzgerald was not finished. By late summer 1939 he was writing *The Last Tycoon.* The work went slowly, but it went. With no income and no savings, Fitzgerald was supporting himself and his family with $250 checks from *Esquire* for the seventeen Pat Hobby stories about a broken-down Hollywood hack.

Through 1939 and 1940 Perkins kept Hemingway informed about the progress of Fitzgerald's novel—carefully obeying Fitzgerald's instructions to keep the nature of the material a secret. Perkins told Hemingway that Scott expects Scribners to bankroll him with an advance, but Perkins cannot justify it. On 19 December 1939 Perkins wrote Hemingway that Fitzgerald was sick, but that it is hard to tell what the situation really is because Scott always hires trained nurses: "I would feel as if it might as well be an undertaker, and even more embarrassing." After a couple of benders, Fitzgerald was again firmly on the wagon. An indication of Fitzgerald's respect for Hemingway's authority, as well at Fitzgerald's sense of isolation from him, is provided by his 6 June 1940 letter to Perkins inquiring about Hemingway's sense of how World War II would go—asking for "at least a clue to Ernest's attitude."

While Fitzgerald was struggling with illness and debt to write *The Last Tycoon,* Hemingway enjoyed his greatest success when

For Whom the Bell Tolls was published in October 1940. His first major work of fiction since 1929, the novel sold more than 270,000 copies in its first year. Hemingway sent his novel to Fitzgerald inscribed "To Scott with affection and esteem Ernest." The ironic

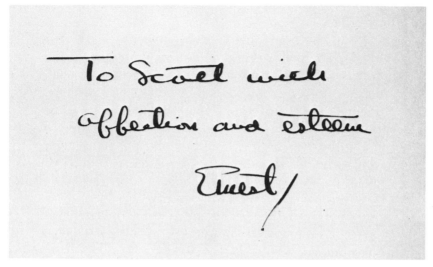

Bruccoli Collection.

reversal of their fortunes since 1925 was painfully apparent to Fitzgerald. In his weekly letter to Zelda of 26 October he commented:

> Ernest sent me his book and I'm in the middle of it. It is not as good as the "Farewell to Arms". It doesn't seem to have the tensity or the freshness nor has it the inspired poetic moments. But I imagine it would please the average type of reader, the mind who used to enjoy Sinclair Lewis, more than anything he has written. It is full of a lot of rounded adventures on the Huckleberry Finn order and of course it is highly intelligent and literate like everything he does. I suppose life takes a good deal out of you and you never can quite repeat. But the point is he is making a fortune out of it—has sold it to the movies for over a hundred thousand dollars and as it's The Book-of-the-Month selection he will make $50,000 from it in that form. Rather a long cry from his poor rooms over the saw mill in Paris.

Fitzgerald acknowledged the inscribed copy with a warm letter of congratulation, obliquely referring to his efforts to complete his own novel:

November 8, 1940

Dear Ernest:

It's a fine novel, better than anybody else writing could do. Thanks for thinking of me and for your dedication.[46] I read it with intense interest, participating in a lot of the writing problems as they came along and often quite unable to discover how you brought off some of the effects, but you always did. The massacre was magnificent and also the fight on the mountain and the actual dynamiting scene. Of the side shows I particularly liked the vignette of Karkov and Pilar's Sonata to death—and I had a personal interest in the Moseby guerilla stuff because of my own father. The scene in which the father says goodbye to his son is very powerful. I'm going to read the whole thing again.

I never got to tell you how I liked *To Have and to Have Not* either. There is observation and writing in that that the boys will be imitating with a vengeance—paragraphs and pages that are right up with Dostoiefski in their undeflected intensity.

Congratulations too on your new book's great success. I envy you like hell and there is no irony in this. I always liked Dostoiefski with his wide appeal more than any other European—and I envy you the time it will give you to do what you want.

With Old Affection,

[Scott]

P.S. I came across an old article by John Bishop about how you lay four days under dead bodies at Caporetto and how I flunked out of Princeton (I left on a stretcher in November—you can't flunk out in November) and how I am an awful suck about the rich and a social climber. What I started to say was that I do know something about you on the Italian front, from a man who was in your

46 Fitzgerald is referring to the inscription; the novel was dedicated to Martha Gellhorn.

unit—how you crawled some hellish distance pulling a wounded man with you and how the doctors stood over you wondering why you were alive with so many perforations. Don't worry—I won't tell anybody. Not even Allan Campbell who called me up and gave me news of you the other day.

P.S. (2) I hear you are marrying one of the most beautiful people I have ever seen. Give her my best remembrance.

This was the last letter from Fitzgerald to Hemingway.

Writing to Perkins on 14 October 1940 Fitzgerald had suggested a theory about Hemingway's marriages: "It will be odd to think of Ernest married to a really attractive woman. I think the pattern will be somewhat different than with his Pygmalion-like creations." This prediction was sound, for Martha Gellhorn's pursuit of her own career led to the breakup of the marriage.

Despite his praise to Hemingway, Fitzgerald had strong reservations about *For Whom the Bell Tolls*. One of his *Notebook* entries reads: "It is so to speak Ernest's 'Tale of Two Cities' though the comparison isn't apt. I mean it is a thoroughly superficial book which has all the profundity of Rebecca." And, comparing his work-in-progress on *The Last Tycoon* with Hemingway's novel: "I want to write scenes that are frightening and inimitable. I don't want to be as intelligible to my contemporaries as Ernest who as Gertrude Stein said, is bound for the Museums. I am sure I am far enough ahead to have some small immortality if I can keep well."

All of his life Fitzgerald had a list-making compulsion. Perhaps because his personal life had been so unstructured, he felt a compensatory need to keep records. The most elaborate attempt was his *Ledger*, which is virtually an autobiography. He would also make lists on single sheets of paper. One of these, dating from the year of his death, is a chronology of Fitzgerald's meetings with Hemingway from 1925 to 1937. At the end of it he noted: "Four times in eleven years (1929–1940). Not *really* friends since '26."

F. Scott Fitzgerald died of a heart attack in Hollywood on 21 December 1940, leaving *The Last Tycoon* unfinished. On the day of his death he told Sheilah Graham that he hoped to write about the war from Europe: "Ernest won't have that field all to himself,

March – aug '25   Paris
Oct '25 – Feb. '26   Paris
Apr '26 – Oct '26   Riviera

One Day in October '28 } 1 in 2½ yrs

Apr '29 – June '29   Paris

Three or four meetings in Autumn 1929
                                    ←——— Two years
One meeting in Oct 1931   ←——— Two years
One meeting in   1933   ←——— Two years
Two meetings in   1937
                                    ←——— Three years

4 Times in 11 years

Four times in eleven years (1929–1940). Not really friends since '26

F. Scott Fitzgerald Papers, Princeton University Library.

then." It is not known how or when in Cuba Hemingway learned of Fitzgerald's death. He did not attend the funeral in Rockville, Maryland, on 27 December. Perkins sent Hemingway an account of Fitzgerald's funeral on the 28th: "I thought of telegraphing you, but it didn't seem as if there were any use in it, and I shrank from doing it."

It has been incorrectly reported that F. Scott Fitzgerald died with his books out-of-print. The truth is just as bad. At the time of his death all nine of his books were in stock—including copies of the 1925 second printing of *The Great Gatsby*. In 1940 all of Fitzgerald's books sold a total of seventy-two copies.

V

Ernest Hemingway outlived F. Scott Fitzgerald by twenty-one years.

Hemingway made no public statement after Fitzgerald's death. He was not among the six writers (Budd Schulberg, John O'Hara, Glenway Wescott, John Peale Bishop, Malcolm Cowley, John Dos Passos) who contributed to *The New Republic* symposium on Fitzgerald in 1941—but perhaps he was not asked.

Perkins kept Hemingway informed of his attempts to salvage *The Last Tycoon* and briefly considered asking Hemingway to complete the novel—which was probably the worst idea the great editor ever had. The idea was quickly dropped, partly at Zelda Fitzgerald's insistence. Her response to Perkins conveyed her feelings about Hemingway without mentioning his name: "May I suggest that rather than bringing into play another forceful talent of other inspiration it would be felicitous to enlist a pen such as that of Gilbert Seldes, whose talent depends on concision of idea and aptitude of word rather than on the spiritual or emotional transports of the author." The final plan was that Edmund Wilson would edit *The Last Tycoon*, which was published in 1941 as an unfinished novel with *The Great Gatsby* and a selection of stories.

The size of the first printing of *The Last Tycoon* is not known, but it was less than 5000 copies. The reviews were receptive; and many critics agreed with Wilson that *Tycoon* would have been

Fitzgerald's most mature work. The judgment that it would have been his masterpiece was not unusual. Stephen Vincent Benet's assessment in *The Saturday Review of Literature* attracted considerable attention: "You can take off your hats now gentlemen, and I think perhaps you had better. This is not a legend, this is a reputation—and seen in perspective, it may well be one of the most secure reputations of our time." *The Last Tycoon* sold slowly but steadily. A second printing was required in 1941; it was reprinted in 1945, 1947, and 1948.

Hemingway was not impressed when he read *The Last Tycoon*. Writing to Perkins on 25 November 1941, he complained of its deadness. Monroe Stahr is good, but Kathleen is unbelievable. Ernest applies to Scott the metaphor that he would later use in *A Moveable Feast:* the dust was off the butterfly's wing, even though the wing could still move. Scott's best novel is *Tender Is the Night,* which has none of the "impossible dramatic tricks that he had outlined for the final book." Scott died inside when he was thirty or thirty-five; *The Last Tycoon* was written after Scott's powers had died, too. Hemingway quarrels with Wilson's selection of stories for the volume: "The Rich Boy" is silly, and "The Diamond as Big as the Ritz" is trash. Ernest is glad the novel is getting good reviews, but a writer who knew Scott can tell that the writing is dead. It is like moldy bacon; if the mold has penetrated, then the meat will taste moldy. Scott was like a pitcher with a dead arm. He got some of his "old magic" into the airplane episode, but there is no magic in the characters. Scott never knew enough about people to write a novel that did not depend on magic.

During World War II Hemingway enlarged his legend. After running a civilian Q-boat operation in Cuba, he went to Europe. Nominally a *Collier's* correspondent, he led irregular soldiers in France, personally liberating the Paris Ritz and Sylvia Beach. In 1944 he fell in love with correspondent Mary Welsh, who became his fourth wife in 1946.

On 17 February 1944 Perkins briefed Hemingway on Wilson's projected Fitzgerald miscellany, which was published as *The Crack-Up*. Perkins never liked the plan and declined to publish the volume. Although Perkins doesn't go into the disagreement in this letter, he was opposed to Wilson's decision to reprint the "Crack-Up" articles—which embarrassed Perkins. The publication of *The Crack-Up* by New Directions was a catalyst for the Fitzgerald revival. It became a key volume for Fitzgerald's admirers and has never gone out of print.

Hemingway wrote to Perkins on 25 November 1944 urging Max to hold Scott's letters for a "definitive book" and not to let Wilson pee them away. Ernest has saved all of Scott's letters about writing, which show his strengths and weaknesses. "I knew him, through some periods, better than anyone and would be glad to write a long, true, just, detailed (all of those I mean in the measure that anyone can do such a thing) account of the years I knew him." Ernest recommends John Peale Bishop as a better editor for Scott's letters than Wilson, who is dishonest and pretentious.

When *The Crack-Up* was published, Hemingway wrote Perkins on 23 July 1945 asking for a copy. Ernest is sorry that he hasn't written about Scott because he knew Scott possibly better than any of the people who are writing about him. But he can't write truly about Scott while Zelda is alive. Ernest insists that Scott would never have completed *The Last Tycoon,* which was really a prospectus for drawing advances. Scott pitched the novel at an "Epic note" that he could not have sustained. He did everything wrong in his writing, but it came out right. Ernest can speak honestly to Max because they both loved Scott and knew his weaknesses. Scott's great flaw was the cowardice that made him live in a dream world. He thought he could have been a great broken-field runner, but Scott had trouble crossing Fifth Avenue traffic. Hemingway's comment on *The Crack-Up* has not been found. If he read all of the volume, he found himself mentioned fourteen times in the "Notebooks" section (see Appendix).

The Crack-Up was followed in 1945 by *The Portable F. Scott Fitzgerald,* with an introduction in which John O'Hara announced: "All he was was our best novelist, one of our best novella-ists, and one of our finest writers of short stories." Hemingway characterized this introduction as "wrapped in O'Hara's old coonskin coat that he never wore to Yale." The Viking Portable series included a Hemingway volume.

Maxwell Perkins died in June 1947.

Zelda Fitzgerald died in a fire at Highland Hospital, Asheville, North Carolina, in March 1948.

Hemingway's first public post-mortem reference to Fitzgerald appeared in the introduction to the 1948 illustrated edition of *A Farewell to Arms,* where "Scott FitzGerald" is included without comment in a list of friends who have died since the novel was published. When Arthur Mizener was working on the first biography of Fitzgerald in 1950, Hemingway responded with eight long letters and granted permission to print excerpts from his letters to Fitzgerald. Hemingway wrote Mizener that he loved Scott very much but never had any respect for him, "except for his lovely, golden, wasted talent." He placed much of the blame for Scott's destruction on Zelda's jealousy of his work and informed Mizener of her complaint about Scott's penis—which Mizener did not use in *The Far Side of Paradise.* Scott's best book is *Tender; Gatsby* is good but over-rated; but *Tycoon* was a scheme for borrowing money. Hemingway also provided Mizener with accounts of the Callaghan bout and Fitzgerald's letter of advice about *A Farewell to Arms.* Hemingway acknowledged receipt of an advance copy of *The Far Side of Paradise* on 4 January 1951, complimenting Mizener on his research and offering to correct the "many errors" when he has time. Hemingway was "sickened" by Mizener's article, "F. Scott Fitzgerald's Tormented Paradise," in the 15 January 1951 issue of *Life.* Writing to Harvey Breit of the *New York Times Book Review* on 17 January, Hemingway described the article as "straight grave robbing" and "all scandal and a nickel's worth of literature." On the 6th of February he wrote Breit that he would like a chance to kill Mizener for his "body-snatching" *Life* article.

Budd Schulberg's novel *The Disenchanted* was published in November 1950, preceding *The Far Side of Paradise* by two months. Schulberg has insisted that Manley Halliday, the hero of *The Disenchanted,* was not intended to be a portrait of Fitzgerald—but a synthesis of several Hollywood writers. Nonetheless, the novel was read as a roman à clef about F. Scott Fitzgerald; and this interpretation was supported by the circumstance that the central action of *The Disenchanted* draws upon Schulberg's experiences with Fitzgerald on location for a movie about the Dartmouth Winter

Carnival in 1939. The close publication of the biographical novel and the biography made Fitzgerald literary news again in 1951.

The biographical interest in Fitzgerald generated a new market for his work. In 1951 Malcolm Cowley edited two volumes for Scribners, *The Stories of F. Scott Fitzgerald* and the so-called "author's final version" of *Tender Is the Night*. Writing to Cowley (who had edited *The Portable Hemingway*) in April 1951, Hemingway assessed the Fitzgerald revival and its spokesmen.

I had the same re-action you did about what a shame it was for Scott not to be around for his own revival. But to be revived by such strange people: First Schulberg, a very nice guy everybody says, and most pleasant when I met him once in Key West, writes something that really balls up everything about Scott and Zelda. I never saw Scott in that stage of his life. But the way Zelda is handled makes the whole thing sort of pointless.

Mizener deceived me completely by his letters. I thought he was a straight guy and then came that unspeakable piece of grave robbery he wrote for LIFE. . .

Poor Scott; what robes, or shroud, he had were torn and sold by very strange people. I hope to hell you will be able to set some things right. As you know only a few of the short stories are good. Gatsby is good and Tender Is The Night is mixed up but absolutely excellent. The Last Tycoon is very good. But it was more a beautifully organized scheme to borrow advances on than a completed novel. I am sure Scott would have fought to complete it. But from what I heard from the people who were with him at the end; especially one man I knew and who told me very detailed things, he was quite incapable of finishing it. But Scott tried hard and did not die from dear old Dartmouth nor on the playing fields of Princeton and I am afraid I think both Schulberg and Mizener are swine; no matter how plausible.

You are a decent man and whatever you do, according to Scott's wishes, about Tender In [*sic*] The Night is ok. People have a choice of reading either version. But that Schulberg-Mizener Axis could well be hanged, head down, in front of any second rate garage.

Despite his outrage at Mizener's treatment of Fitzgerald, Hemingway confined his protests to private letters. His comments on *Tender* reiterated the ambivalence of his original judgments. The characters were imperfectly conceived, but the novel succeeded because of the brilliance of the writing. In July 1951 Hemingway reacted to Cowley's editing of *Tender* in accordance with Fitzgerald's second guess that his novel had been flawed by its flashback structure: "I'll read the new Tender Is the Night if you think it is better. But I thought its lack of chronological order was one of the things that redeemed it from the mixing of Scott and Gerald, Zelda and Sara, and gave it that fine mixed-ness of a Frozen Daiquiri. Scott had, most of all, charm and in this book more than any other. I think there is a danger in over-dissecting charm. . . . But Tender Is the Night was a damned beautiful and most sad book and I thought it only achieved the unity it had by the extraordinary mixing it received in Scott's mixing machine. . . ." Two months later, in September, Hemingway again analyzed for Cowley Fitzgerald's imperfect understanding of people and his inability to create true characters.

> As you know Scott was one of the worst writers who ever wrote prose. . . . Scott caught the surface and the people that he knew or met with a fine brightness. . . . But Scott would mix up (as in Tender I.T.N.) himself and Zelda with Gerald and Sarah and they were very different. He got balled up inventing from mixtures of opposites in people instead of inventing from his knowledge of people themselves. How could he ever know people except on the surface when he never fucked anybody, nobody told him anything except as an answer to a question and he was always too drunk late at night to remember what anybody really said. . . . Maybe the strain of trying to out-write himself ruined him, as you said. But he was a true rummy when I met him when I was married to Hadley . . . that was one of his big problems, that and Zelda, and cowardice, and ambition and love of earning money which meant social, economic, and for a while, he figured, artistic success. . . .

In 1951 Scribners sold 29,821 copies of Fitzgerald's books; in 1958 Scribners' sales broke 50,000; and in 1960 the total was 177,849 copies. Hemingway's response to the books and articles about Fitzgerald was a mixture of incredulity and annoyance at the inaccuracies he found. Writing to Charles Scribner in 1951, he characterized Fitzgerald as a liar and a drunk with the talent of a frightened angel. While trying to dissuade Charles Fenton from writing a study of the Hemingway apprenticeship in 1952 he commented, ". . . a good man is dead and a garrulous fool speaks for him, and no amount of Mizener makes it come alive." When the *New York Herald Tribune Book Review* asked Hemingway for a list of books he liked in 1951, he provided six titles he would have liked to read if they had been published—including *"Longevity Pays: The Life of Arthur Mizener* by F. Scott FitzGerald" and *"The Schulberg Incident* by F. Scott FitzGerald." In March 1953 Hemingway commented to Charles Poore: "Scotte was a good friend of mine. He could not stay the course for many reasons. But I have never written about them except the one reference in "The Snows of Kilimanjaro" and would hate to have a slighting reference now." When Harvey Breit was collaborating with Budd Schulberg on the play version of *The Disenchanted,* Hemingway wrote Breit in August 1954 describing Zelda's destructive influence on Fitzgerald—including her complaint about Scott's penis. Scott was an Irish rummy; he seemed to enjoy humiliating himself and the people with him. "But when, after one awful night when I had to give a large sum to the doorman at the Plaza to square something really awful Scott had done, I told him I couldn't ever go out and eat with him any more unless he would promise not to be horrible to people, or make an effort not to be anyway, he was able to write that thing about how he spoke with the authority of failure and I with the authority of etc. and so we would never be able to sit at table together again."

In the fifties Ernest Hemingway became the most famous and successful living author in the world. John O'Hara's *New York Times* review of *Across the River and into the Trees* (1950) began: "The most important author living today, the outstanding author since the death of Shakespeare, has brought out a new novel. . . . The author, of course, is Ernest Hemingway, the most important, the outstanding author out of the millions of writers who have lived since 1616." Although *Across the River and into the Trees* was a critical disaster, Hemingway reclaimed his championship in 1952—if he had ever lost it—with *The Old Man and the Sea*. The news that Ernest and Mary Hemingway were missing in an African plane crash in January 1954 made the front pages all over the world; and Hemingway was able to read his own obituaries. In October 1954 Ernest Hemingway was awarded the Nobel Prize for Literature.

Hemingway began work on a memoir of Fitzgerald in 1957 for the 100th-anniversary issue of *The Atlantic Monthly* but dropped it because, he explained to Breit, he didn't want to betray Scott. This project probably initiated work on a book of Paris reminiscences he had been considering for some time, which was posthumously published as *A Moveable Feast* in 1964.

Ernest Hemingway shot himself at Ketchum, Idaho, on 2 July 1961.

VI

"Madame, it is always a mistake to know an author."
—*Death in the Afternoon*

F. Scott Fitzgerald and Ernest Hemingway loved to dramatize themselves—to act out their own mythologies. One played the ruined genius; the other played the titan. Both roles met with public acceptance.

Writers become identified with their material. Since failure is a major theme in Fitzgerald's fiction, readers have become conditioned to regard him as the objective correlative for failure. The concerns of Hemingway's fiction are endurance-courage-cojones, which he embodied in his well-publicized nonliterary life. It became increasingly difficult to differentiate the public Papa from the private writer. Whether or not he sought publicity, he provided good newspaper copy and was an excellent camera subject. His photos show the ebullient Hemingway engaging in sport or war, or the bearded patriarchal Hemingway looking wise and indomitable. Hemingway's photos, above all, present a man enjoying himself because he seems to be getting all there is out of life. The most frequently reproduced photos of Fitzgerald are of the young man doing a dance step with his wife and daughter—or the middle-aged man at forty-three with gray skin and unhappy eyes, wearing a checked jacket and a knit tie, looking like the ghost of F. Scott Fitzgerald.

"Scott Fitzgerald was a failure as a success—and a failure as a failure," remarked restaurateur Prince Michael Romanoff. He did not know Fitzgerald well, but the observation epigrammatizes the standard approach to Fitzgerald's career: his self-proclaimed failure. Yet Fitzgerald's achievements would constitute a triumphant career for most writers. In twenty years he published four novels, a play, some 160 short stories, a score of essays—and left a major novel unfinished at his death. Although Fitzgerald denigrated his stories as hack-work, they include some of the best in American literature: "The Rich Boy," "May Day," "The Diamond as Big as the Ritz," "Babylon Revisited," "The Last of the Belles," "Winter Dreams." He was not a careless writer who dashed off an occasional masterpiece during binges. Fitzgerald was an alcoholic, but his benders alternated with periods of sober hard work. He was not a quick and sloppy writer; his manuscripts show that even for the disparaged *Saturday Evening Post* stories there were layers of careful revision. For his novels Fitzgerald was accustomed to rewriting—not just polishing—in proof. He was as much a craftsman as Hemingway was. Yet Hemingway's name evokes literary dedication, whereas Fitzgerald's evokes irresponsibility. The publicly drunk Fitzgerald was an embarrassment, but the working Fitzgerald was unobserved. No writer writes eight hours a day, every day. Most writers are happy with two or three good hours. Hemingway occupied his non-writing time with sport, and made it appear that hunting and fishing were related to his aesthetic. He had the ability to make everything he did seem to have something to do with literature. Hemingway radiated confidence. Fitzgerald became identified with defeat—largely through his own public statements. A shrewd careerist would not have published the "Crack-Up" essays. Hemingway attributed Fitzgerald's public humiliations to a love of defeat. A better explanation is provided by Fitzgerald's symbolic quality, for he seemed to embody the national mood. So intense was his identification with his times that he assumed the roles which the prevailing mood required. During the Jazz Age he symbolized youth and confidence. During the Depression he symbolized thwarted expectations and remorse. Although Fitzgerald was a failure in his own judgment and in the eyes of a public that needed a totemic failure figure in the Thirties, evaluations of Fitzgerald's failure provide gauges of his achievement.

Fitzgerald could not accommodate success or failure. In his 1937 essay "Early Success" he wrote, "The compensation of a very early success is a conviction that life is a romantic matter." For the romantic the value of an experience is inseparable from the circumstances that attend it: the meaning of the moment is the moment itself. In *This Side of Paradise* Amory Blaine dreams of "being made the youngest general in the world"; and Fitzgerald observes that "It was always the becoming he dreamed of, never the being." It is hyperbolic to claim that Fitzgerald deliberately threw away his early success, but he was unable to shape a career from it. Neither could he accept failure. At the end of his life he was incapable of fading out as a Hollywood hack.

In "The Crack-Up" Fitzgerald refers to his once-held conviction that "life was something you dominated if you were any good." The obvious and awful irony is that he was not a dominator. Indeed, he was a born hero-worshipper who sought models for his conduct. The greatest hero Fitzgerald found was life-dominating Ernest Hemingway. The intensity of Fitzgerald's identification with Hemingway is hard to understand. Perhaps the best clue to Fitzgerald's feelings about Hemingway is provided by the phrase "Ernest who was an equeal and my kind of idealist." Fitzgerald saw Hemingway as someone who shared his values—which is puzzling at first. Fitzgerald was a great believer with a "heightened sensitivity to the promises of life." Hemingway confronted an antagonistic world in which there was nothing to believe except courage. Stay around and they would kill you. The Hemingway code provided a method for enduring in the absence of traditional beliefs. *Il faut d'abord durer* became his chief commandment. There is a malevolent presence in Hemingway's work, and the Hemingway hero copes with it by substituting courage and discipline for the lost beliefs and comforts. The concern of Hemingway and his heroes with craftsmanship provided a way of imposing certain controls over life. The value of the experience is in how well it is performed. The apparent absence of emotion in Hemingway's early work fooled many readers into classifying him as an anti-romantic writer. But the insistence on personal standards, the self-testings against private gauges, the courage required to confront a hostile world, the controlled despair—in Hemingway these formulate an anti-romantic romanticism.

Fitzgerald was able to identify with Hemingway as "my kind of idealist" in literature. At every stage of his career, from obscure apprentice to graybeard master, Hemingway spoke with conviction about his dedication to his craft—as well as the irresponsibility of other writers. Fitzgerald responded to the intensity of Hemingway's commitment, which allowed Fitzgerald to feel that he was among the insiders of American literature. As an artist Hemingway embodied the standards of discipline and dedication that Fitzgerald aspired to. One of the many paradoxes of Fitzgerald is that he cherished high goals for his work while dissipating his creative energies. As a Princeton undergraduate he had remarked that he wanted to be one of the greatest writers that ever lived. So did Hemingway, whose ambitions manifested themselves in competition with all writers, living or dead. When he spoke about beating Stendhal or retaining his championship, he meant it: "I won the title in the twenties and defended it in the thirties and forties. I am not afraid to defend it in the fifties." Yet Hemingway did not progress from strength to strength. His best work was done before he was thirty, and he produced only one major novel—*For Whom the Bell Tolls*—after 1929. Nonetheless, he spoke with the confidence of success. Everything he did, everything he wrote, became important because he was Ernest Hemingway.

At the time of their first meeting in spring 1925 Fitzgerald was at the peak of his powers, having developed from the inconsistent brilliance of *This Side of Paradise* and *The Beautiful and Damned* to the control of *The Great Gatsby*. A year earlier he had announced to Maxwell Perkins: "I want to write something *new* —something extraordinary and beautiful and simple + intricately patterned." *The Great Gatsby*—published before Fitzgerald was twenty-nine—fulfilled that ambition. Instead of building on the achievement of *Gatsby*, Fitzgerald was unable to concentrate on sustained work for the next seven years. Despite his well-earned playboy image, Fitzgerald suffered guilt over his dissipations.

Maybe he needed to feel guilty. The example of Hemingway made Fitzgerald feel both more and less guilty. If Hemingway's dedication to writing shamed Fitzgerald, it also allowed him to feel that he shared it. "The test of a first-rate intelligence is the ability to hold two opposed ideas in the mind at the same time, and still retain the ability to function," Fitzgerald stated in "The Crack-Up."

Neither Hemingway nor Fitzgerald influenced the other's writing. Hemingway grudgingly accepted Fitzgerald's advice about cutting; and Hemingway read the work-in-progress on *Tender Is the Night*, but there is no record of his reactions. Although they discussed problems of technique and the aims of fiction, it requires ingenuity to suggest evidence of imitation. By the time they met, their styles and material had been fixed.

The literary relationship between Fitzgerald and Hemingway existed on the basis of shared ideals about the value of literature. Their work was utterly dissimilar in style, themes, material, and technique. Fitzgerald was a traditional stylist who wrote a modulated lyrical prose. Although some of his social material seemed sensational in the early twenties, Fitzgerald was a rather old-fashioned novelist with conventional standards of conduct. He was an intrusive author in the sense that he was a storyteller who commented on the story as he told it. Fitzgerald never wrote a straight first-person novel. When he employed narrators in *The Great Gatsby* and *The Last Tycoon*, they function as novelists. Fitzgerald's stance as a storyteller required an authorial voice. Hemingway, however, had difficulty breaking away from the first-person narrative of *The Sun Also Rises* and *A Farewell to Arms*. His early fiction tries to eliminate the authorial presence, conveying the impression of experience reported as directly as possible. In his time Hemingway was regarded as an experimental writer. His style represented a new method in its abrupt rhythms, understatement, and objectivity.

One thing shared by the work of Fitzgerald and Hemingway—although achieved by different methods—is a concern with "the way it was." Writing to Perkins in 1934 about himself, Hemingway, and Thomas Wolfe, Fitzgerald observed: "What family resemblance there is between we three as writers is the attempt that crops up in our fiction from time to time to recapture the exact feel of a moment in time and space, exemplified by people rather than things. . . ." Hemingway utilized things much more than Fitzgerald—and named them. There is a reportorial quality in Hemingway's work that is absent from Fitzgerald's fiction. Hemingway's technique—in his early work, at least—was to let the observed detail convey emotion with no authorial analysis. Fitzgerald was more concerned with evoking and analyzing the feeling of an experience than with recording detail. As he advised his daughter, "But when in a freak moment you will want to give the low-down, not the scandal, not the merely *reported* but the profound essence of what happened at a prom or after it, perhaps that honesty will come to you—and then you will understand how it is possible to make even a forlorn Laplander *feel* the importance of a trip to Cartier's!"

The Fitzgerald/Hemingway friendship was lopsided. It was not one-sided. *A Moveable Feast*—written thirty years after the events—does not present an accurate view of Hemingway's feelings about Fitzgerald during the early years of their friendship. *Feast* is not the young Hemingway's diary; it is not a record of the way it was at the time. The mood is that of an aging giant looking back from the perspective of what he has become. His letters to Fitzgerald in the Twenties are more trustworthy, for *Feast* was written during Hemingway's darkening years. While his letters do not show that Hemingway held personal respect for Fitzgerald, they do reveal his affection and his high opinion of Fitzgerald's talent. In 1932, after the friendship had become mostly a memory, Hemingway was still insisting, "He is the great tragedy of talent in our bloody generation."

In a literature crowded with bad drinkers, Fitzgerald may have been the worst. Alcohol turned him foolish, destructive, truculent, childish. His drinking behavior cost him the respect of many friends. The response was strong in the case of Hemingway, who had developed drinking conduct as a test of manhood. Another Hemingway test of manhood that Fitzgerald failed was the ability to control women. Distrusting the destructive or castrating power of women, Hemingway was sickened by what he regarded as Zelda Fitzgerald's domination of her husband. He was particularly disgusted by her interference with Fitzgerald's work. Hemingway's work came before all things.

At the same time that Fitzgerald was capable of exasperating conduct, he possessed enormous charm and had the ability to make people believe he was really interested in them—because he was. Looking back at himself as he had been in the Twenties, Fitzgerald commented, "Once I believed in friendship, believed I *could* (if I didn't always) make people happy and it was more fun than any thing." Fitzgerald had a compulsion to help people. He was extremely generous about other writers and did not manifest any sense of competition with them. It could be argued that his generosity was a form of ego-gratification; but his benefactions were real. When they first met, Hemingway needed Fitzgerald's help to advance his reputation, and Fitzgerald joined the cadre of writers who were promoting Hemingway's career. Indeed, Fitzgerald wrote to Perkins about "Hemmingway" some seven months before they met.

Like many other ambitious young writers, Hemingway cultivated the good will of influential literary figures and accepted all the help he could get. Breaking into print and developing a reputation is such a chancey process that ambitious young writers learn to develop influential supporters. (Fitzgerald had come to Scribners under the aegis of Shane Leslie.) Not only was Fitzgerald's interest in Hemingway's career helpful, but Fitzgerald—sober—was an extremely attractive friend. "Endearing" is the word Hemingway applies to him at this time in *A Moveable Feast*. Moreover, Hemingway was an excellent judge of writing and assessed Fitzgerald's talent very high, although he was not greatly impressed by Fitzgerald's achievement. Hemingway thought that *This Side of Paradise* and *The Beautiful and Damned* were silly and regarded Fitzgerald's short stories as trivial. *The Great Gatsby* impressed Hemingway in 1925, but he later revised his opinion of that novel.

Hemingway was ruthless in his judgment of people. As a man who lived by a strict code of conduct, he had no empathy for weakness. Yet he needed friends and made close friendships easily—possessing the ability to draw people to him and make them feel that they had been accorded membership in an exclusive cult.

Membership did not carry tenure, for the friends of Hemingway were subject to permanent banishment. As he grew older he found it better to have nonliterary friends. He was more comfortable with stooges than with equals. Nonetheless, for five or six years Hemingway made allowances for Fitzgerald, forgiving his alcoholic misconduct and mending breaks in the friendship. After Hemingway became in his thirties the most famous living American author, Fitzgerald's friendship became a nuisance. As Archibald MacLeish wrote of Hemingway, "Fame became of him."

One of Hemingway's basic doctrines was that "A man can be destroyed but not defeated." There was a long time when its application to Fitzgerald would have seemed remote. Now most of the evidence is in, and it turns out that Fitzgerald was, in his own way, undefeated: "I am not a great man, but sometimes I think the impersonal and objective quality of my talent and the sacrifices of it, in pieces, to preserve its essential value has some sort of epic grandeur."

Appendix

Notebook References to Hemingway Included in *The Crack-Up**

P. 99 I really loved him, but of course it wore out like a love affair. The fairies have spoiled all that.

_____

147 Ernest—until we began trying to walk over each other with cleats.

_____

189 Ernest Hemingway, while careful to avoid cliches in his work, fairly revels in them in his private life, his favorite being Parbleu ("So what?") French, and "Yes, We Have No Bananas." Contrary to popular opinion he is not as tall as Thomas Wolfe, standing only six feet five in his health belt. He is naturally clumsy with his body, but shooting from a blind or from adequate cover, makes a fine figure of a man. We are happy to announce that his work will appear in future exclusively on United States postage stamps.

_____

125 They have more money (Earnest's wisecrack)

_____

174 As to Ernest as a boy—reckless, adventurous, etc. Yet it is undeniable that the dark was peopled for him. His bravery and acquired characteristics.

_____

* These entries have been transcribed from Fitzgerald's Notebooks. The *Crack-Up* texts are unreliable.

[163]

176 Nevertheless value of Ernest's feeling about the pure heart when writing—in other words the comparatively pure heart, the "house in order."

176 That Willa Cather's poem shall stand at beginning of Mediaval and that it shall be the story of Ernest.

177 Just as Stendahl's portrait of a Byronic man made *Le Rouge et Noir* so couldn't *my* portrait of Ernest as Phillipe make the real modern man.

177 But there was one consolation:
They could never use any of Mr. Hemingway's four letter words, because that was for fourth class and fourth class has been abolished—
(The first class was allowed to cheat a little on the matter.)
But on the other hand they could never use any two letter words like NO. They *had* to use three letter words like YES!

178 Didn't Hemmingway say this in effect:
If Tom Wolfe ever learns to separate what he gets from books from what he gets from life he will be an original. All you can get from books is rhythm and technique. He's half-grown artistically—this is truer than what Ernest said about him. But when I've criticized him (several times in talk) I've felt bad afterwards. Putting sharp weapons in the hands of his inferiors.

181 I talk with the authority of failure—Ernest with the authority of success. We could never sit across the table again.

200 Very strong personalities must confine themselves in mutual conversation to very gentle subjects. Everything eventually transpired—but if they start at a high pitch as at the last meeting of Ernest, Bunny and me their meeting is spoiled. It does not matter who sets the theme or what it is.

224 Most Pleasant Trips
. . . .
Auto Ernest and I North
. . . .

Notebook Entries Not Included in *The Crack-Up*

Ernest Hemingway and Ernest Lubitsch—Dotty "We're all shits."*

People like Ernest and me were very sensitive once and saw so much that it agonized us to give pain. People like Ernest and me love to make people very happy, caring desperately about their happiness. And then people like Ernest and me had reactions and punished people for being stupid, etc., etc. People like Ernest and me———

Ideas on Fear as being removed as well as profit motive. We know the latter can—but the former. Some day when the psycho-an are forgotten E.H. will be read for his great studies into fear.

An inferiority complex comes simply from not feeling you're doing the best you can—Ernest's "drink" was simply a form of this.

It is so to speak Ernest's 'Tale of Two Cities' though the comparison isn't apt. I mean it is a thoroughly superficial book† which has all the profundity of Rebecca.

I want to write scenes that are frightening and inimitable. I don't want to be as intelligible to my contemporaries as Ernest who as Gertrude Stein said, is bound for the Museums. I am sure I am far enough ahead to have some small immortality if I can keep well.

Snubs— . . . Ernest apartment.

Parallel of Ernest's and French conversation as opposed to Gerald and me and U.S.A. emotional bankruptcy.

Do you know what your affair was founded on? On sorrow. You got sorry for each other. (Did Ernest borrow this one?)‡

Day with a busy man. Combine the day of Ernest's pictures, the man of genius episode, [Cuppy and McKisco.]

---

* Hollywood director Ernst Lubitsch and Dorothy Parker.
† *For Whom the Bell Tolls.*
‡ Printed in *Crack-Up,* p. 196, with parenthetical comment omitted.

Ernest taking me to that bum restaurant. Change of station implied.

Bald Hemingway characters.

Tom Fast's story of Ernest.

Ernest and "Farewell to Arms"—producer story.

Bradogue* steals Hemingway

Ernest would always give a helping hand to a man on a ledge a little higher up.

* Bradogue became Brady in *The Last Tycoon*.

A Note on Sources

F. Scott Fitzgerald's letters to Ernest Hemingway are at the John F. Kennedy Library, Waltham, Massachusetts. Most of these letters are included in *The Letters of F. Scott Fitzgerald,* ed. Andrew Turnbull (New York: Scribners, 1963). Hemingway's letters to Fitzgerald are at the Princeton University Library, as are the Charles Scribner's Sons archives, which include Maxwell Perkins' correspondence. Most of the Fitzgerald/Perkins correspondence has been published as *Dear Scott/ Dear Max,* ed. Jackson Bryer and John Kuehl (New York: Scribners, 1971). Hemingway's letters to Charles Poore and Arthur Mizener are at the University of Maryland Library. Portions of these letters have been quoted or facsimiled in auction catalogues; see *Hemingway at Auction,* ed. Matthew J. Bruccoli and C. E. Frazer Clark, Jr. (Detroit: Bruccoli Clark/Gale, 1973). Hemingway's letters to Malcolm Cowley are quoted from Sotheby Parke Bernet catalogue #4035 (25 October 1977). Hemingway's letters to Harvey Breit are at the Houghton Library, Harvard University. A standard tool for Hemingway research is Charles W. Mann and Philip Young, *The Hemingway Manuscripts: An Inventory* (University Park and London: Pennsylvania State University Press, 1969).

Carlos Baker's *Ernest Hemingway: A Life Story* (New York: Scribners, 1969) is the standard biography. There are two biographies of Fitzgerald: Arthur Mizener's *The Far Side of Paradise* (Boston: Houghton Mifflin, 1951) and Andrew Turnbull's *Scott Fitzgerald* (New York:

Scribners, 1962). Photos of the Fitzgeralds and their friends are repro-duced in *The Romantic Egoists: A Pictorial Autobiography of F. Scott and Zelda Fitzgerald*, ed. Scottie Fitzgerald Smith, Matthew J. Bruc-coli, and Joan P. Kerr (New York: Scribners, 1974). Two important memoirs of Paris in the Twenties are Morley Callaghan's *That Sum-mer in Paris: Memories of Tangled Friendships with Hemingway, Fitzgerald, and Some Others* (New York: Coward-McCann, 1963) and Harold Loeb's *The Way It Was* (New York: Criterion, 1959). A recon-struction of the events behind *The Sun Also Rises* is *Hemingway and the SUN SET*, ed. Bertram D. Sarason (Washington, D.C.: Bruccoli Clark/NCR, 1972). An account of Gerald and Sara Murphy is Calvin Tompkins' *Living Well Is the Best Revenge* (New York: Viking, 1971). Two articles examining Fitzgerald's editorial efforts on Hemingway's novels are Charles W. Mann and Philip Young, "Fitzgerald's *Sun Also Rises*," *Fitzgerald/Hemingway Annual 1970*, and Mann's "F. Scott Fitzgerald's Critique of *A Farewell to Arms*," *Fitzgerald/Hemingway Annual 1976*.

About the Author

MATTHEW J. BRUCCOLI, Jefferies Professor of English at the University of South Carolina, is a leading authority on F. Scott Fitzgerald and John O'Hara. He has written or edited some thirty volumes in the field of American literature. Among his recent books are *The O'Hara Concern: A Biography of John O'Hara* and *The Romantic Egoists,* a pictorial autobiography of F. Scott and Zelda Fitzgerald, which he edited with Scottie Fitzgerald Smith and Joan P. Kerr. He is now working on a collection of John O'Hara's letters and a new collection of F. Scott Fitzgerald's letters for Random House.

Dr. Bruccoli, a graduate of Yale University and the University of Virginia, lives in Columbia, S.C., with his wife and four children. He is a partner in Bruccoli Clark Publishers.